T0374307

Slices of Life in Hawaii

Volume 1

J. Arthur Rath III

iUniverse, Inc.

New York   Bloomington

Slices of Life in Hawaii Volume 1

Cover photographs: *Top row left to right:* Barack Obama, page 288; Soot
Bredhoff, page 82; Colleen Hanabusa, page 1. *Second row left to right:* Kuhi
Suganuma, page 200; Aaron Mahi, page 16. *Third row:* Sumida Watercress
Farm, page 94.

iUniverse books may be ordered through booksellers or by contacting:

iUniverse
1663 Liberty Drive
Bloomington, IN 47403
www.iuniverse.com
1-800-Authors (1-800-288-4677)

Because of the dynamic nature of the Internet, any Web addresses or links
contained in this book may have changed since publication and may no
longer be valid.

ISBN: 978-1-4502-3519-8 (sc)
ISBN: 978-1-4502-3520-4 (ebk)

Printed in the United States of America

iUniverse rev. date: 6/3/2010

"Sing me a song of the Islands,

Where hearts are high and the moon is low."

Mack Gordon and Harry Owens

Harry Owens and his Royal Hawaiian Band

theme song, circa 1940

Contents

Introduction

Slices of Life in Hawaii includes emotional responses to stories told to me by a variety of people in this extraordinary place known as Hawaii. Some flow from my personal experiences, conveying wonder and awe about these storied islands and their people.

This is a collection of individual postings, not a continuum. Please skip around for flavors, perspectives, lightheartedness, and evocations.

The Islands' mixture of people—ethnicities and cultural experiences—creates a wealth of stories resonating emotionally with islanders and non-islanders alike.

Reading certain *Slices* may seem similar to listening to older family members' remembrances; some incorporate a sense of passing time and change while relating what remains the same. Each appeared in HawaiiReporter. com, the online news journal.

I see myself as a channel—a person gratefully helping others share their tales. And I'd enjoy hearing from you for some "Slices," too! They could go online first, then maybe in volume 2.

J. Arthur Rath III
imua@spamarrest.com

Growing Up

Many of these stories occurred in rural Hawaii, circa 1930s–40s.

Except for downtown Honolulu, contiguous neighborhoods,

And main cities on all islands . . .

Life in the Territory of Hawaii was lived in isolated rural areas,

Or in thin pockets of small communities,
Surrounded by large expansions of land.

The ocean was never far away.

Colleen ready for school.

1.

Waianae's Colleen Hanabusa

Waianae Sugar Plantation started in 1878 with 20 local Hawaiians and a few Chinese laborers. Six years later it fostered Hawaii's largest settlement outside of Honolulu.

Its sugar mill, one of the finest in the kingdom, employed 500 Japanese. Two of them, the Murodas, were Colleen Hanabusa's maternal great-grandparents.

Great-grandfather Muroda worked in the cane fields and gained fluency in Hawaiian, becoming an unofficial village wise man because he could communicate and pass on advice from his wife. She also worked in the fields and was Waianae's midwife.

Because midwives knew something about healing, their counsel was sought in old-time Hawaiian community life. While Mrs. Muroda had two children of her own, she maintained an interest in the children she helped bring into the world, including her six grandchildren. Connections of all types mattered. It was easy to be regarded as *ohana*—as part of the family.

Colleen's maternal grandfather Muroda, the plantation's carpenter, built wooden flues—the vital lifelines that carried water from Makaha Valley down into the arid plains.

The Hanabusa side of Colleen's family showed a flair for entrepreneurship. Her paternal great-grandfather Hanabusa made and sold tofu, and her grandfather fished from his boat, selling his catch to the plantation store. The love of fishing passed down the generations, becoming the source of a shared bond between Colleen and her father, Isao.

Colleen started fishing as soon as she was able to hold a pole. "My dad was prone to seasickness, so he and I fished from the shoreline while grandpa went beyond the reef," she said.

They caught *mamo, papiopio, nenue,* and *menpachi.* On moonlit nights they fished off the reefs for *aweoweo* and *weke.**

A *nenue*'s sharp teeth can cut a line, so father and daughter Hanabusa used wire leader when fishing for them. Colleen recalls that they were ready for other gifts of the sea as well.

"As we tramped in the water, we'd sometimes see tasty *namako*—sea cucumber; the Hawaiian name is *loli.* We'd quickly peel off their brownish exterior and apply lemon juice so they wouldn't shrivel. We came prepared for those encounters."

Her mother, June, once worked as a butcher's assistant and knew about cuts of meat. "She bought wonderful things," Colleen said. "Gourmet cuts, actually. But they were inexpensive because many people didn't know about them. And she appreciated the value of bones; we never lacked for good stock and good soup. Grandma tried to make sure dark German rye bread was available at soup time."

Isao Hanabusa worked for Gaspro before World War II started. Owned by the Renton family, it was a large local company, suppliers of acetylene, oxygen, and other gases. Isao was classified as "essential" to the war effort because Gaspro supplied gases for airplanes. "Dad remained close to the wonderful people in the company. At age 87 they still had him working with the board of directors."

After the war, Isao achieved his dream: Owning a service station in Waianae. He built a home from a series of little cottages behind Hanabusa Gas Station; he and June worked around the clock to serve customers, eventually adding auto parts to their offerings.

Five year-old Colleen now had two little brothers, so her maternal grandparents said, "Come live with us," since they were in the same area.

All throughout history grandparents have raised children while parents supplied the basic needs for survival. Hawaiians call it *"hanai,"* meaning to raise, sustain, and nourish another's child. Some sociologists believe that children raised by grandparents tend to be more understanding and grateful than other children. And that's my opinion, too, because I was one.

In the next story, Colleen's contemporary, Nola Nahulu, describes growing up in Waianae:

. . . Attending Japanese language school at the end of the public school day,

. . . Participating in community activities,

. . . Enjoying the friendly cheer of neighbors.

Colleen, who had similar experiences, adds: "While in grammar school, I learned to enjoy reading mysteries and historical novels.

"But what I enjoyed most was zipping around the village on little metal roller skates. There were no sidewalks, so we skated on the raised asphalt highway. I liked to go fast; that meant I fell down a lot. I would pick embedded bits of asphalt from my knees. You don't mind a little blood if you're having fun."

While in the eighth grade, Colleen told her parents she wanted to attend a private school—maybe even an all-girls school!

She took the entrance exam for St. Andrews Priory, and the scrappy kid from Waianae did just fine, even though it turned out she was suffering a painful case of mumps at the time.

In the days before freeways, going to and from school was a long trip into town, but she had a family support system to get her there and back.

At the Priory, in the crisp atmosphere of a proper Episcopal girls school, the sweet-but-tough little Buddhist from the country flourished. She became student body president and was known as one of "the brains."

Honolulu Weekly publisher Laurie Carlson was quoted as saying about her classmate, "If the Priory ever produced a Tita, it was Colleen."

"Tita" is Hawaiian slang having a number of different meanings and connotations. In Colleen's case, it meant she was a catalyst for action—unafraid to be heard and to shake things up when something needed to get done.

With a family history running four generations deep and touching three different centuries, Colleen Hanabusa didn't just *grow up* in Waianae: She became inculcated in an ethos of courage, forthrightness, and loyalty.

Since she was a child, her parents reminded her, "Waianae has been good to our family. People there respect you. You are part of them, you understand them, and you belong to them."

She earned as a neighborhood descriptor:

Colleen belongs to us; she's one hardworking, smart Tita!

*Fish names in English: Sergeant fish, small pompano, soldier fish, "big eye," a redfish, surmullet or goatfish.

Left photo, left to right, Chiyoko Nozaki Nahulu, Thomas Kaleilehuaopanaewa Nahulu.
Right photo, left to right, Linda and Nola Nahulu.

2.

Belief in Us: Nola Nahulu

Once upon a time, Waianae was a gentle place where my sister Linda and I lived among a conglomeration of plantation workers' families who exemplified the saying: "It takes a village to raise a child."

After Waianae Elementary School closed for the day, Linda and I rode our bikes to the Japanese Language School held at the Waianae Hongwangi where our Aunty Morime was a Sunday school teacher. Our Japanese grandmother was pleased we received this supplementary education.

Dad was the "doorman" and we both helped our Aunty Morime sell movie tickets.

Waianae had two movie theaters in the early 1950s–60s. It was another opportunity to exchange smiles and small talk with friendly neighbors.

Waianae was a postcard-perfect example of a Hawaiian countryside filled with the mix of our plantation community.

There was Pililaau Park and pavilion where Fourth of July races, Halloween Parades, a May Day Celebration, and Lei Contests were held, among other events.

We even had our own song contest at Waianae Elementary School. It was safe then and people looked out for each other. Whatever their ancestry, everyone was regarded as "family."

Rural Waianae had limited resources, so when ballet classes were offered at the Waianae Hongwangi by Mrs. Sugano (which later moved to Pililaau Park), we "checked it out" and stayed with it.

We continued when it moved to Ewa Plantation. Even when we were boarders at Kamehameha, Mom picked us up every Saturday to attend ballet classes at the Kalihi YMCA. We were fortunate enough to take private piano lessons from Mrs. Hamilton and Mr. and Mrs. Graham, who taught out of their homes in Waianae.

Being accustomed to humble circumstances, we were astounded when Dad and Mom bought us a piano!

No matter what the sacrifice, they always made the effort to give us, their precious girls, "Life Experiences"!

We were never nagged, just encouraged. We even had the chance to study abroad in Japan for a month—before even Mom and Dad got to go!

Locals thought he was taking a huge risk when Dad decided to build duplex houses close to our home. Dad and Mom were grounded on one fundamental belief: They would do whatever was necessary to make sure that we would have life opportunities and the option to attend good colleges.

Building and renting houses would help to make that possible.

"Our land will be working for education," Daddy explained.

Being surrounded by love and dedication was a powerful incentive for us to do our best. Linda and I sought to live up to our parents' belief in us. Innately, I think we still do.

Beginning as seventh graders, Linda and I were both boarders at Kamehameha School. We both received a strong general music foundation from Mrs. Keaka at Waianae Elementary School, but it was at Kamehameha that our love of choral music developed.

We were both fortunate to have been members of the Concert Glee Club beginning in our sophomore year.

Thanks to our parents' sacrifices, both of us graduated from private liberal arts colleges. I attended Whitman College in Walla Walla, Washington, majoring in psychology. Then I came home to receive a masters in music education from the University of Hawaii (UH) at Manoa. Linda went to Macalester College in St. Paul, Minnesota, where she majored in cultural anthropology.

Linda also came home and earned an MD degree at John A. Burns School of Medicine, University of Hawaii. She serves there as associate professor of child and adolescent psychiatry. Our parents' examples instilled our insights and commitment to our community and people.

In 1982, when Dorothy Gillett retired, another blessing was showered on me. Dorothy said, "Hey Nola, why don't you take over my Hawaiian Chorus?"

Dorothy was a 1931 graduate of Kamehameha School for Girls. Retiring from teaching at the UH in 1982, she received a Lifetime Achievement Award for her contributions to Hawaiian choral music.

She was still directing the university's chorus. She also directed the all-male Kamehameha Alumni Glee Club and arranged its music—a job she did for love for 40 years!

Dorothy asked me to take the Glee Club on when cancer made it impossible for her to continue. Thanks to my parents, I had gained the necessary training. From Dorothy I received the opportunities to use it.

Now it is our turn to give back:
I direct the Hawaii Youth Opera Chorus that fosters personal and social development and a lifetime of music appreciation for ages 5 to 18. I also work with singers of all ages as part of the university's affinity for community outreach and am given many opportunities to participate in musical activities within the community as part of the Hawaii Opera Theatre and through Kawaiahao Church, as well as the Association of Hawaiian Civic Clubs.

Linda has done much research on attention deficit hyperactivity disorder, especially with our Hawaiian children. She works with children's' families as well and prepares medical students for that challenge.

Our parents, Thomas Kaleilehuaopanaewa Nahulu and Chiyoko Nozaki Nahulu, gave us the chance to learn what to do.

Linda and I appreciate the opportunity to honor them by attempting to inspire others. Smiling faces from the old community who nurtured and "helped to raise us" will never be forgotten.

Me ke aloha pauole . . . Nola e Linda Nahulu

[Nola A. Nahulu has devoted herself to educating Hawaii's children beginning in 1978 at Our Redeemer Lutheran School, the Kamehameha Schools, and the University Lab School. Since 1982 she has directed the Hawaiian Chorus at the UH Music Department. She is currently choral director for Pearl Harbor Hawaiian Civic Club, Kawaiahao Church, Hawaii Opera Theatre, and Ka Waiola o Na Pukanileo, and has served as the Executive Director for the Hawaii Youth Opera Chorus since 1986. In her spare time she sings with No Kaliko, an a cappella trio devoted to Hawaiian choral music. With her family she owns Bete Muu, manufacturer of classic muumuu. In honor of her many activities, she was named Hawaiian of the Year in 1987 by the Association of Hawaiian Civic Clubs.]

3.

Overcome Bad Times: Terry Plunkett

Because of turmoil I experienced growing up in Hawaii, I encourage young people to learn about becoming good providers, spouses, and parents.

They need to:

- Be able to appraise themselves and set realistic and attainable goals.
- Establish a realistic achievement plan.
- Coalesce health, social, and spiritual components within their lives.

I am neither a philanthropist nor am I an intellectual who is long on theory and short on practice. I am just a part-Hawaiian fellow who experienced childhood domestic mayhem, was shunted from place to place, and who somehow learned to survive and manage.

Some fellows my age might be reflecting on the sunset of their life. I am presenting a sunrise through personal management training organized into teaching modules called "Life." As grassroots as anything could ever be, "Life" is my acronym for Living Independently For Everyone. I am sowing the seeds.

I reached this point from experiencing the downside while growing up in Hawaii.

Who teaches anyone to be a good spouse or parent? Well, maybe loving, enlightened parents, but not everyone has that capability. Here's my story.

I was three years old when my parents divorced. My mother married four times. My father's new wife was mentally disturbed.

I was being forced to adjust to the latest husband or the insanity of my father's wife. After five years of this, my grandparents—who lived in Laie—took me in. Then they adopted me.

Grandpa was an epileptic who worked on Honolulu's piers.

He had a fit while on the job; young Mormon men restored him, then nursed him back to health and into Mormonism.

That became his and grandma's focus in life, leaving me kind of on my own until Mr. Allen Bailey, from Kamehameha School for Boys, appeared at Kahuku School and invited me to become a boarding student. Going there was the salvation for kids like me.

I was 5 foot 3 1/2 inches, weighed 185 pounds, and in my sophomore year became a varsity starting lineman on our championship football team.

By my senior year I dropped down to 155 pounds. I'd fallen in love with a schoolmate's sister—that'll give you an idea as to how fragile my psyche was.

I was on the honor roll, but football meant as much to me as converting to Mormonism did to grandpa. My responses during a University of Hawaii entrance interview went this way:

Describe a room: A locker room.

Your worst day: Missed kicking an extra point.

Most influential person: Football coach Mr. Tom Mountain.

The Korean War was on. I joined the U.S. Air Force, was sent to Japan, and played football on the championship Johnson Air Force Base's "Vanguards," along with the Menendez Twins, who'd starred at Farrington High School.

While at the University of Hawaii, I met my wife Darlene. We raised two daughters and a son. Our emotional life has been smooth sailing. I call that "mutual good management" and *wonderful luck!*

I taught at Kailua High School, was recruited by the telephone company, and spent 15 years working in Hilo. Management training and counseling became my life's work, along with helping at a center for gifted and talented Native Hawaiian children. By going to night school, I earned a master's degree.

Having hands-on, frontline experience as a business and human relations pragmatist, I realize that *business management skills can coalesce into life-management skills.*

My uncertainties were caused by lack of parental stability. I realize how prevalent that same situation is now, especially when times are tough. My school then made it a point to recruit kids from every island who were in troubled situations and who might have potential. That was my Blessing.

Most "special programs" these days seem to focus on high achievers or nonachievers.

What about mainstream Hawaii? What about kids like me—the hoi polloi? Hard times will be especially challenging to them. That's what I learned while growing up in Hawaii.

Aaron Mahi

4.

Sweet Memories

Somewhere I read serious oenophiles declare, "No wine before its time." Aging improves that product's quality for the true connoisseurs who savor it.

Growing up in Honolulu, I learned, "Go to the bakery at the right time and enjoy pastry at its most sublime."

Buying oven-fresh pastry was the secret.

I acquired this valuable information while attending Kalakaua Intermediate School. At 6:00 a.m., nearby on King Street, was when apricot Danish came out of Liberty Bakery's ovens. Going to school early meant the joy of a post-breakfast snack of tart, warm, flowing apricot pudding surrounded by soft, sweet pastry!

Liberty took apple donuts from its oven at noon. These were *malasadas,* Portuguese-style sugared donuts without holes, filled with warm, sweet-sour apple filling. Having 25 cents lunch money in my pocket meant I could visit the bakery three times a day to savor magical creations when flavors and textures were best.

At 2:30, when school ended, regular donuts were ready—warm and at the peak of freshness and flavor.

Before they cooled, the texture was feathery-light, the sweet flavor just slid down your throat. We ate them right outside the bakery and went home bouncing and sugar-high exhilarated—laughing and chattering.

At 6:00 p.m., fresh bread came out of Liberty's ovens. Our family stopped there on the way home from church. Then we'd gather around the kitchen table to eat the oven-warm white bread with cheese, and we'd drink hot chocolate.

After teaching classes at Roosevelt High School, I left to arrive at Liliha Bakery by 1:30 p.m. when, out of the oven, came the sugar palms—these were like puff cookies. Cinnamon twists were also ready. You had to be there to do the twists right; once they cooled down they were put in the refrigerator. That somewhat hardened the fluffy pastry.

They were just perfect at 2 p.m.! Cinnamon melted on hot twists like a glaze.

Danish pastry exited the oven at about the same time. The apricot syrup flowed and the dough was soft and moist—the perfect time to eat it. Warm Danish nestles so seductively on the palate.

At 1:30 p.m., on days when I wasn't teaching, friends and I waited for the long johns to come out of the oven lightly sprinkled with powdered sugar.

These were filled with absolutely *the best custard* one could ever taste, encased in a soft and smooth and shapely exterior. The warm pastry had a nice crispy initial crunch—it melted like butter within our mouths. Umm!

Timing was everything. The sensations of eating fresh-from-the-oven long johns were different from what customers experienced after the product was cooled and refrigerated. They turned into "usual" bakery goods—not the special treats *we* experienced.

To savor all those sensations in one day meant seven stops in about 12 hours. Of course, we never made them all, but we always knew what was due to come out of the bakery ovens at what time. We planned accordingly.

Honolulu was such a friendly place, most locals knew bakeries' schedules—*for enjoying pastries at their most sublime.*

I left to study in the eastern United States and in Europe, traveled widely as a band, orchestra, and singing conductor, and became a musical scholar and composer.

I enjoy Vienna along with its world-famous fancy and elegant pastries. But as Dorothy said in *The Wizard of Oz* movie, "There's no place like home!"

Home in Honolulu, we youths experienced pastry excitement and were so hyperactive that calories didn't count. Local bakery owners greeted us as we came in the door, spoke to us by name, pointed knowingly at their clock, and *just grinned!*

They enjoyed our dedication to what was being prepared a few steps from the sales counter. We kids were their loyal, enthusiastic epicureans.

[Aaron Mahi is the former conductor of the Royal Hawaiian Band, director of Honolulu Symphony Pops and the Kamehameha Schools Men's Alumni Choir. Mahi sings traditional Hawaiian songs Sunday evenings at the Marriott Waikiki Hotel with George Kuo and Martin Pahinui. He is trilingual—English, Hawaiian, and German—and received the Golden Ring of Honor from the Association of German Musicians and Order of Merit of Germany.]

Colbert Kalama

5.

What 'Aloha' Means

A general sameness prevails in many of my stories of Hawaiians growing up. Our experiences were pretty similar, yesterday.

Population changes made that life a memory storehouse. Hawaiians are a minority in their homeland, so many others share shrinking resources once so freely available. Population density and content has changed. Not everyone knows Hawaiians.

Here's an exemplar.

Colbert A. K. Kalama, a heavy-chested, slim-waisted man, developed his physique from canoeing and paddling. He does it competitively and participates in local races.

Shortly after becoming a Kamehameha Schools' trustee, he told alumni:

"Anxiety is always good, it keeps you on your toes. It's one of the reasons I race."

21

Describing his childhood, he said, "Elders in the community helped make me mellow, as did genial Dad."

The seventh of eleven children in his family, Colbert was born in Kailua, lived in a 900-square-foot home, and was raised within a "whole community"—meaning a neighborhood having a broad ethnic mix.

He'd catch fish with a throw net and then drop off some of his catch at neighbors' homes.

He remembers the fun of riding down grass hills on cardboard boxes from a local store.

Kalama knew "Daddy Bray," exponent of Hawaii's old-time ethical and religious values and author of *The Kahuna Religion of Hawaii.*

He explained, "Daddy said 'Aloha' referred to the spiritual side of life within old-fashioned Hawaiians." He told us to remember their use of that word as an acronym for harmony in life:

*A: **ala**, watchful alertness*

*L: **lokahi**, working with unity*

*O: **oiaio**, truthful honesty*

*H: **haahaa**, humility*

*A: **aahonui**, patient perseverance*

"Elders like Daddy enjoyed perpetuating old-time knowledge."

Kalama remembers Eddie Kamae, ukulele virtuoso, singer, and composer.

"Kamae used his long fingernails to make sounds such as no one had ever heard come from a ukulele."

After completing Kailua High, Kalama was the first in his family to attend college. The Community Foundation helped to pay his way.

"The dream of furthering my education wasn't just my own, it was my family's as well," he explained.

Colbert graduated from Western Oregon College, majoring in economics, and from the Pacific Coast Banking School, where he also served as a faculty member.

He taught at Kailua High School and in the Honolulu Community Action Program.

Kalama said most Hawaiian cultural traditions he encourages came from his mother. "She taught us old values, stressed positive aspects of things.

"My father was generous with everything to everybody. He was a happy man! Dad conveyed old-time Hawaiian-style equanimity.

"We cared for each other and for our neighbors."

The Kalama family has reunions about four times a year. "We've blond-haired, blue-eyed kids in our family—diversity is my background."

He experienced no difficulty in launching his career at First Hawaiian Bank: "I had the desire and was confident it was the right place for me."

Kalama speaks animatedly, smiles readily, eyes sparkle brightly, his body language is expressive. Seeing him shrug his massive shoulders is a treat.

"I always look up to a *kupuna*—an old-timer—because they have knowledge," he explained.

His attitude caused us elders to gaze fondly at him; people feel comfortable with affable Colbert in charge.

[Executive vice president with First Hawaiian Bank, Colbert Kalama is responsible for the bank's Oahu region and manages its more than 30 branches on the island. He is also First Hawaiian's personal banking and small business banking segment manager. Kalama has been a trustee of the University of Hawai'i Foundation, and the Queen Liluokalani Children's Center, and he served with the American Bankers Association and the Government Relations Council Bankers Roundtable.

He also served with the Polynesian Voyaging Society, Pacific Islanders in Communication, and the Hawai'i Institute for Public Affairs. A trustee of Kamehameha Schools, he is vice president of the board.]

6.

Kauai Boyhood

These recollections are from friends who grew up on the Garden Island prior to statehood. The country living they describe was experienced over 25 years before developers and realtors began welcoming new arrivals with ballyhoo: "Town houses, luxury condominiums, gated communities, and Gentlemen's Estates. Own your share of Paradise!" Things are a bit different now.

Wailua Beach was an extension of our front yard. Dad waded straight forward for 25 yards, threw out a fish line, walked back to our front porch, tied his fishing pole to it, relaxed, and waited until the line started moving—the signal a fish had taken the bait.

The fishing line burned streaks on his arm as he pulled in 100- and 125-pound *ulua* (pompano). He considered those battle marks as badges of courage. Dad did no pussyfooting over his masculinity.

He'd hang big fish tails on our open garage so passersby could see them displayed. These were prideful trophies.

Dad cut up the *ulua,* kept a share for us, and gave the rest to neighbors.

In Kauai, in the late 1930s to early 1940s, we experienced general neighborliness: We cared for others and kids were safe.

We grew sweet potatoes and raised chickens on our 1 1/2 acres. Dad and I caponized roosters to make them fat for eating.

We grew clusters of banana plants, ten mango trees, lots of plumeria trees—blossoms were available to anyone wanting to pick fragrant flowers for lei.

Three kids were in our immediate family—country Hawaiian-style living augmented that—and area kids were considered part of everyone's family.

Both of my parents worked; my duties included washing the rice for dinner.

We kids could choose the kind of food we wanted to eat—Chinese? Filipino? Hawaiian? Japanese? Just show up for dinner at a specific ethnic home. Kids were always welcome. Everyone seemingly loved us; we could wander far and wide safely—a wonderful way to feel!

Should anyone be foolish enough to harm a kid, they'd experience swift local response such as Shirley Jackson described in her short story, *The Lottery.* No chance to plead their case before a local judge. He'd throw the first stone!

At that time on Kauai it was unthinkable to be anything but convivial and kind to youngsters.

Bicycles took us everywhere. We'd knock down ripe mangoes from trees, travel along the tracks and pull ripe sugarcane off the railroad car—it was warm, juicy, and sweet. Fun to see who could spit chewed pulp the farthest.

Kokee, in Waimea Canyon's vicinity, was the Eden our parents described. We'd wander, pick plums, let juice drip down our chins.

Fishing adventures took us far from the back door where Dad cast his line. We traveled up to six or seven miles, used throw nets and spears, dove for half a day. If experiencing a bonanza, we shared our catch with neighbors along the way home. It's what Dad taught us.

Mormon community members kept their kids together and encouraged athleticism. We played baseball, basketball, and barefoot football against other Mormon teams and competed against Catholic Youth Organization teams. Competitive experiences would prove invaluable in high school and college.

Dad was a mighty and emotional baseball player—he took the game seriously. The regular announcer was absent when we were up against a major rival and some loud wise guy began making his own caustic commentary. Dad coldcocked him with one punch.

Polite mouths were expected in friendly Kauai, or. . . .

That's in contrast to a recent event. Photos in newspapers and TV footage showed Kauai residents standing, yelling, protesting against Governor Lingle. She was attempting to speak to a Kauai community group during its Super Ferry fury.

Men wore the bills of their baseball caps backwards, doing so to protect sun from shining on the back of their necks—hoping not to be known as Jeff Foxworthy characters.

If any Hawaiians were present, they were out of camera range—probably fearing Tutu's wrath should her *moopuna* be shown shouting at our governor. Uncouth!

7.

Small Kid Time: By Marion Lyman-Mersereau

Mom had a "squid eye." She learned as a girl, from an old Hawaiian man, how to hunt for the camouflage experts in the coral reefs, a glass box was her guide, a metal spear her weapon.

Family friends had a beach house at Punaluu and they would invite us to join them for a weekend or let our family use it a few times a year. My brothers and I would spend hours snorkeling over the rocky bottom inside the reef where we would explore coral heads and see *manini, menpachi,* jaw jutting moray eels and short spine *wana.*

At low tide mom would put on her tabis, get her glass box and spear then walk slowly toward the outside reef. She'd stop to carefully examine any coral head that might house a cleverly hidden eight-legged chameleon.

I would snorkel not far from her.

When she found a *he'e** she speared it then called me to get my dad, who swam his lazy, long arm stroke to where my mom stood. She awkwardly held onto the spear while she kept her distance from the tentacles that climbed the metal shaft like tendrils of a vine reaching toward sunlight.

I stayed a few feet back and watched the speared, slippery creature turn colors, my eyes as wide as large tiger cowries in my swimming mask.

When my dad came to the rescue he would calmly take the creature off the spear, bite the eye, killing it instantly, turn it inside out, throw it over his back and swim in. When he reached the beach his back was covered in red marks where the many suckers of eight tentacles had stuck to him.

He'd pound it, dry it, and smoke it. So *ono,* the *he'e* my mother caught and my dad retrieved.

My aunt and uncle had a cabin that they built in the 1930s a few miles from Ka'ena Point. We had many family gatherings there, in that most isolated part of this island.

We beach combed in the morning, snorkeled in the afternoon and played cards or read into the evening. So many fishermen surf casted in that rough, rocky ocean that it was always like Easter when we snorkeled only the eggs we hunted were gray, lead fishing weights of various shapes and sizes. We would have two fists full weighing us down after about an hour of diving. I can remember running up the beach to unload my heavy lead treasures, mixed with the occasional cone shell or cowry, on the towel where my mom sat and assumed the role of lifeguard with her sister.

One day my brother followed a spear fisherman who was swimming toward the beach, he was admiring the many fish that dangled on the fisherman's line that he pulled far behind him.

My aunt loudly, but calmly alerted my brother to swim quickly to the beach. My mom yelled at my other brother and me to also swim quickly to the beach.

I remember standing by the edge of the water where we watched an eight-foot nurse shark swim by. This confused me because they also called it "the man in the gray suit." At age nine I'd never known a male nurse.

*Actually, "octopus," not squid.

8.

Adults and Kids Talked

Little girls are sprinkled with magic dust. If we're lucky, some rubs off on us.

Dayna Pacarro received the nickname of "Sweetie," blossoming into what she'd always been.

This three-year-old grinned at anyone passing by the walkway leading to her parents' Alewa Heights home. Too young to attend school, she waved and talked with neighbors. Kids were safe those days.

Early verbal abilities often predict future mental capabilities; you recognize what the Pacarro family had here.

She tells it: "Youngest of five children, I learned to speak up or be left out of conversations. Our family was pretty verbal. Being the littlest didn't mean being the last to be heard."

She says, in her rapid-fire style, "I began answering the phone for Daddy's business before I started going to school. People seemed to enjoy talking with me."

Who knew when people said, "Thanks Sweetie," it would become her name?

"We had a very loving family—relatives enjoyed calling me 'Sweetie.'"

At this point I mentioned a truism: A childlike side never fully leaves a woman. That's why Maurice Chevalier's song, "Thank Heaven for Little Girls," is so appealing.

She answered, "My parents sang that song to me."

Sweetie explains how her career seed was planted.

"I went to the Star of the Sea High School and grew up listening to Hal Lewis, who was known as 'J. Akuhead Pupule.' He set the pattern for morning disc jockeys in Honolulu. Michael Perry and Larry Price 'carry on' in this style.

"Am I going too fast for you?"

Though struggling, I answer, "No, I can keep up."

"I wanted to be a pediatrician because I love working with kids, but at the same time I wanted to go into broadcasting."

I asked, "What made you think broadcasting might be right for you?"

She stifled a giggle. "Our freshman history teacher wanted us to do a history report in the style of a newscast. Pretending I was KHON's Joe Moore, Hawaii's top-rated broadcaster, I began with:

"'And in the news today . . .', then imitated his flexible, confident, warm-voiced delivery from the incisive, detailed script I had written. It was embedded with smoky adjectives."

"Smoky?"

"Yeah, real hot!

"The teacher's eyes almost glazed over. He said, 'You are *really* good at this.'"

After class he said, "You're a natural. This is what you should do. Become involved in drama, do stage work."

"He was excited over 'his discovery' and was a good mentor."

Living in Honolulu meant a chance to become Miss Hawaii National Teenager and Miss Hawaii U.S. Teenager. Those pageants awarded Sweetie college scholarships.

"At 16 I met Bradley Johnson, who attended St. Louis School; he was my high school sweetheart. We have three beautiful children: Kaniau, Courtney, and Ikaha Johnson. Brad is a career Air National Guardsman.

"Before all that happened I headed to the University of Portland, in Portland, Oregon, a four-year Catholic institution. The ten years or so it would take to become a pediatrician seemed a little extreme at this point, so I returned to Hawaii and finished at Chaminade College.

"Things went pretty fast: I married, had a child, and still finished college four years after graduating from high school.

"I decided I would be 'Dr. Mom—D.M.'—instead of 'M.D.'

"Everyone freaked out when they heard I was pregnant and said, 'What are you going to do? You're losing all your dreams? This'll end everything you'd planned.'

"I said, 'I'm pregnant, not dead. I'll do all I set out to do.'

"I took one semester off, went back to school, and still graduated in four years. My high-school sweetheart and I have been married for over 21 years."

Sweetie used a top-rated radio station personality's speaking pace: high-energy, tight, bright, to the point, no dead air; focused.

"I served as an intern at KHON, mentored by Kirk Matthews, Nestor Garcia, Ann Botticelli, and many others. Then I applied for a job opening at KSSK, two weeks after graduating from Chaminade. I was hired on the spot by Linda Coble, news director. I met Larry Price and Michael Perry, we had a nice talk, and they began introducing me to others as 'their new associate who will start tomorrow at 5:00 a.m.'"

Sweetie continued her bio: "Twenty years with KSSK. You name it, they let me do it.

"I presently produce the three-hour variety show broadcast Saturday mornings, working with top talent.

"I continued my education, picked up a real estate license. Now I practice pediatric medicine at home and read a lot.

"Being a continuing reader is rudimentary to achieving higher levels of education. I learned that in the Catholic schools I was fortunate to attend."

How to summarize her slice of life? With swirls! Community service is a big thing for Sweetie's station. She works with scores of groups and visits high schools to present awards to coaches.

Our conversation reawakened imagery of a little girl in an innocent time, sitting on steps, eager for an exchange with friendly neighbors.

It was an impression Hollywood projected when times were bad:

. . . Shirley Temple's cute optimism lifted spirits as Americans staggered under the Great Depression.

. . . Indomitable Judy Garland defeated wicked witches on the road to Oz when American GIs faced the inevitability of horrid-filled World War II journeys to Berlin and Tokyo.

Thank heaven for little girls!

Do we listen to our girls as carefully and as nonjudgmentally as Sweetie's parents, family, and friends did? This helps listeners experience and encourage lives they'll influence and feel good about themselves.

9.

Nanakuli's David Kaahaaina

Members of Honolulu's Prince Kuhio Club asked me to introduce him as its *outstanding* member.
Friends find him *inspiring* as well.
He is a quiet man,
Always dependable,
Not pretending he's grand,
His skills are meaningful.

A true kamaaina,
David Kaahaaina.

Eldest of seven Hawaiian Homelands' *keiki,*
4-H, Boy Scouts, sells newspapers—not too shaky!
Gathers *limu,* fishes for the family to eat;
Hawaiians have hard times; they're not on "Easy Street."

Instead of boring stuff, seeming ephemeral,
Outdoor classes turn bugs and clouds into new friends.

His teachers' calm manners cajoled the destructive,
Turning all students into being constructive.
At Nanakuli, his teachers taught him these styles
That foster Dave's persona—which always beguiles:
Calmness, never at odds,
Loving Nature and God.

Kamehameha School for Boys sends an invite:
"Join us on the hilltop, because you are so bright.
You can eat and live here as an eighth grade border."
Dave responds: "I can't do that in such short order:

I want to graduate first from Nanakuli."
This signaled KSB he'd not be unruly.

Ninth-grade Dave, youngest of sixty-five new brothers,
Esteems role models of upperclassmen others.
Earning his fame in four years, he is out the door:
Now family breadwinner for "go to the store."

Those skills gained at school make him real hirable.
Now, to explain what makes Dave admirable:

He is a quiet man, always dependable,
Never thinking he's "grand," three things commendable:

First Is Family
He holds jobs in Navy's Public Works employment,
Comprising many skills for maintained deployment.
(Secret government work,
Its details I must shirk.)

Second Is God

Working on what is seen, with faith in the unseen.
Sacred Hearts' Catholic tradition is his gleam:
Credo in Unun Deo . . .
Patrem omnipotem,
Factorem coeli et terrae,
Visibilium omnium
Et invisilium.

Twenty-years service to Catholic charities,
Around this island, improving facilities.
Elder services and policy making,
Notre Dame Club member—moving and shaking.

Third Is Country

"Don't fight in Korea," is what the draft board said.
"You're deferred to support your large family instead."
Excused from Army service for two years or more,
David chooses, instead, to devote thirty-four!

As a National Guardsman he quickly excelled,
Achieved responsibility—as if propelled!
Andretta knew, when they married, he'd stay in it:
Their lives revolved around keeping that commitment.

Lieutenant-Colonel, Retired, honored highly,
Was invited into Kuhio Club by pal "Smiley"—
That's Richard Jackson, sitting proudly over there
Among school brothers and sisters—you know from where!

The reason we chose Dave for honor and "Hooray!"
Is his genius on Kamehameha Day.
He is "the float person," making it all appear:
Designs, builds, supervises (rewards crew with beer).

He explained the concept so simple and brilliant:
"Because *he* was the king,
Let's cause his strength to ring!
"Show his power—the man portrayed as one who can!
Straight-forward, total male.
Message? <u>He</u> will not fail!
Dave is our class' leader,
The school meeting greeter.
Each quarter, Chinese food
Gives us a mellow mood.

Sends cards to lift Birthday hearts,
Tells us when one departs.
Makes visits to our school,
Chatty news is his rule.

Lucky for us, Andretta's and David's scions
Are twins David, Kerstin, and daughter Kenwyn;
Six grandkids, two great-grandkids, I'm not denying:
Because this family's fame will keep the flag flying!

My honor to tell you,
A real kamaaina;
We all love him so true—
David Kaahaaina.

10.

Richard Jackson's First Priority

They expect to see us twice every week,

We always take turns exchanging the treat,

Watching carefully as they move through rooms:

Smiling, wearing Anna Miller costumes.

We've been to the gym, now it's time to eat.
Pounds off, calories on, our steady beat.

I've been long away from Hawaii Nei,
My friend explains why things turned out this way.
He's what you could call "A Real Hawaiian"—
Sense of duty, tradition, and bloodline.

Insight on the local values he knew,
Plugged in since boyhood, they sustained him through.

43

Work in school office, paid his tuition,
Being track team captain showed his fruition,
In senior year went to classes halfway,
Hawaiian Electric job rest of day.
At noon, teacher drove boys to the city,
Back to school? Up to their ability.

HRT bus part ways to Kalihi,
Missed shuttle? Hour's walk—not *manini*.
Rain and shine, up steep Kapalama Heights,
Steadily forward: step, slip, and some slides.

Track man moves fast, dining schedule conform,
Must change to be there in school uniform.

No college because mother needs support,
So, Hawaiian Electric's his career port.
Hawaii's filled with stories like this:
Kupuna helped by their one-time kids.

Across the Pali, see electric lines?
Precariously there his survey team climbs,
Steadily up there, steps, slides, and some slips,
Almost a lifetime of making those trips.

He tied all together with a long rope,
Lifeline in case they slip down a steep slope.
Big Samoan's placed to anchor the end,
Slip? Digs in his heels: he's everyone's friend!

Kids' ambitions and Hawaii's costs though
Meant finding more ways to bring in dough.

Weekends he prepares big lavish luaus.
Imu-cooked pig and plenty of *laulau*s.
He becomes a popular Hawaiian chef,
And guitarist—plays all keys on the clef.

Skillfully his fingers slip and they slide,
Smoothly from his throat sweet melodies glide.
His Hawaiian voice is rich and mellow,
Modestly, "I'm just a local fellow."

Home life revolves around raising the boys,
That done, volunteers to give others' joys.
"Community was good, now we'll serve it,"
So dedicated, he becomes a hit.

Civic club honor, being exemplary,
His old-time values prove contemporary.

Life changed for his friend and former neighbor,
Divorce, home lost, and injured from labor:
Lives across the island in a tool shed,
Crippled, part-time work yields some Daily Bread.

My friend plans Sundays "Old Neighbor Hooray!"
Long drive, he departs early in the day,
Breakfast, lunch, companionship his Sabbath,
My friend's wife understands his kind of gift.

He calls himself "Just a local fellow."
Looking with awe, wish I were as mellow.

For sixty-five years have I known this man,
Perspectives he shares to gain as I can:
From my words, posture, looks, he can observe
That life's just thrown me another swift curve.

"You're seeming somewhat sad today," he sighs.
Envied empathy: *Oh to be so wise.*

11.

Learning to Read

My teen-aged uncle helped me explore books having lots of words on a page. With his aid, Hans Christian Anderson's enchanting fairy tales weren't insurmountable, nor were the Brothers Grimm's scary ones.

I waited on the front porch for him to return from school, then became his shadow until he handed me a book and settled me down close to his desk.

"What's this word mean?" I asked as Uncle Sam did homework. He attended Punahou School and always had lots of studying to do.

He wrote the word in a notebook before acting it out.

Uncle Sam would quiz me on words in that notebook: "I'm helping to build your vocabulary," he'd say. He grinned broadly as I mimicked his mnemonic "hooks."

Whenever I found a new word, our exchanges were similar to this:

"Uncle Sam, what's 'resound'? This sentence reads:

"Rapunzal let her sweet voice resound."

"Resound is to fill a place with sound—similar to an echo."

He locked it in my memory by shouting *resound!* in his cupped hands, making it "ring."

Uncle Sam explained:

"An echo reflects sound waves from a surface back to the listener.

"I'll take you to the empty Kaimuki Reservoir. Yell into it, your voice will echo (raising his cupped hands for another demonstration) . . . *and resound!*"

Another time, I asked "What does 'creep' mean? I thought it was an 'icky' person. Here's how this story goes:

"Creep in, said the witch, and see if the oven is heated properly. Let me show you how."

Abruptly falling to the floor on his knees, Uncle Sam lifted the desk chair overhead with both hands. Pretending to shuffle under, he explained:

"I'm the witch creeping into the oven."

Abruptly, he shoved the chair to the floor: BANG! This dramatized Gretel's slamming the oven door behind the crafty witch—and then baking her into gingerbread!

His severe acne made him shy; Uncle Sam came home right after school. He stuck around on weekends, never begrudged my trailing him constantly.

During our tandem explorations of the Brothers Grimm's Fairy Tales I learned about deep malevolence, that heroes and heroine can become infinitely happy forever—and that my dark, very Hawaiian-looking uncle was never at a loss for words.

Lt. Samuel Koa Lyman was in General Patton's Armored Corps and was decorated for heroism during the Battle of the Bulge. His middle-name, "Koa", is the Hawaiian word for "soldier." Uncle Sam's up there in Punchbowl Cemetery.

12.

Hawaii Boy's First Shabbos

Hawaii was not as diversified in the 1940s as now. Oh sure, neighbors and people of varied cultures and faiths sometimes mixed socially such as at a family's baby luau in celebration of the baby's first birthday. (This big event is a holdover from Hawaii's time of high infant mortality. A baby's making it to one year was a reason to celebrate after germs for measles, chicken pox, and more arrived in Hawaii from the outside world.)

As another story describes, neighbor country kids were always welcome at the dinner table, but generally, ethnic groups kept religious traditions to themselves. It's how things were then. Living in Honolulu you experienced strata.

Eating festive ethnic foods today has more meaning than tasting ritual soups and sweets from the past. It is a way of assimilating wisdom about something to be preserved. The Italian word for wisdom, *sapienza,* comes from *sapia,* Latin for "taste."

"I taste therefore I know," as in the words of an anthem, "Oh Taste and See," by Ralph Vaughan Williams, the famous twentieth-century English composer. I first sang it among Episcopalians in Saint Andrews' Cathedral:

One meaning of the Christian rite of Communion—of eating Christ's body and drinking His blood—is that this food becomes a path to enlightenment.

I found similar associations with religion and food in an Orthodox Jewish home. It happened while I was learning about mankind's universality.

When attending college in the eastern United States, I spent a spring break in Johnstown, N.Y., with Edward Rosenthal's family. Ed was a Jewish upperclassman; he took me home because I was from Hawaii and had no place to go. We played basketball in the Young Men's Hebrew Association gym (YMHA); I had never been in such a place.

Except for boys wearing caps and those having a long curl, it was what I was used to in the downtown Honolulu YM C A.

Johnstown and nearby Amsterdam and Gloversville were then the center of America's glove-making industry. I took a tour of a leather glove factory and learned to appreciate how exacting and demanding this old-world craft was. (Philip Roth provides beautiful descriptions of the glove-making craftsmanship Europeans brought to America in his Pulitzer Prize book, *American Pastoral*.)

I knew nothing of the culture in my host's home, had no idea what kind of food we would eat, and was delighted by variety, quality, and quantity. Over the course of my spring break I remember being served roast chicken, brisket of beef, gefilte fish, leek soup, meatballs, sautéed chicken livers, and potato latkes.

On Friday, Mother Rosenthal baked challahs, special loaves of braided bread. Whole loaves were placed on the table at Friday evening's Shabbos celebration. We held hands, sang at the dinner table, and ate ritually broken bread. Ed told me it was a reminder of the double portion of manna that descended from Heaven every Friday during the forty years Jews wandered in the desert before they reached the Holy Land.

He explained, "When the manna fell to the ground it remained fresh, for it was covered by a layer of dew below and above it. That's why we place a cloth underneath the challahs and a special napkin over them." During the Rosenthal's Shabbos everything was part of a ritual.

The family welcomed the Sabbath that evening with the song, "Sholem Aleichem."

Mr. Rosenthal recited a poem describing the perfect wife "Whose husband and children praise her as the source of their happiness. It is because she fosters knowledge and good deeds in her husband and children."

These thoughts were similar to words from "The Book of Proverbs" that along with other Kamehameha School students I recited at Princess Pauahi's burial place, Mauna Ala in Manoa, on Founder's Day.

He took his first sips of wine at the blessing. He did a ritual washing of hands and blessing of the bread. Then we started eating.

I was used also to having a cap on my head as the men did, since I was still a freshman and it was required. Wearing my college's beanie at the dining table allowed me to fit right in.

The person passing the wine chalice at Episcopal Communion services only allowed me a sip. But the Rosenthals filled my goblet almost as fast as I emptied it. This made me very jolly.

Ed showed me the family's *pushkas*—containers for charities. "Money, even a few coins, should be put into these every day," he explained. I added my loose change in daily, wanting to fit in.

We had three Shabbos meals in one day. During the first two we were actually hungry; by the time of the third meal we weren't, but did partake, and had song, wine, and rejoiced while fulfilling God's commandment that we eat at least three meals on Shabbos.

"It is not the food that draws us to the table, it is desire to carry out His precepts—the rituals," I was told.

Mr. Rosenthal explained, "The Shabbos candles light up the house and every member of the family with the light of the Torah. This guides them safely along the path of life that is full of dangerous pitfalls." I was beginning to read Robert Frost's poetry then, so what he said made perfect sense to me.

Everyone sang songs of praise throughout the meal. They gave me a printed copy of the words so I could chime in when we came to repetitious parts.

There were recitations and songs and ever-changing dishes of food. There seemed to be a reason for everything. Ed told me, "Fish have no eyelids, so that their eyes are never closed; so too are the eyes of the Lord open at all times to watch over those who fear Him."

Everything was tasty. I really liked the kugel—noodle pudding—it rested my palate from all the wine.

I was becoming exhausted from so much food and a bit dizzy from my never-empty wine glass. But hearing that there would be no cooking in the house tomorrow, I helped myself to more food, having learned earlier from an Italian family with whom I'd spent Thanksgiving, that a good appetite correlates with a good disposition. I certainly wanted to be as jolly as these folks.

Mr. Rosenthal went to the neighborhood delicatessen for Sunday nourishment because "Mrs. Rosenthal would not be cooking."

Sunday was an open house day: Friends stopped by to enjoy what was laid out on the dining room table: whitefish salad, lox (salmon), herring, sliced corned beef and roast beef, coleslaw, potato salad, huge dill pickles, assorted bagels, cream cheese, rye bread, horseradish, and several types of delicious mustards. That was my introduction to a traditional Jewish home.

What I gained became part of my education away from home. It expanded my appreciation about how life can be lived.

Lachaiam!

13.

Always Youthful

Higher education can extend youthful thinking,
optimism, and joy:
Life is a continuum,
Studies endure the long run,
Through a good share of our life
Such times continue to thrive.
Youth: Eyes of the beholder,
Even while we grow older.

Hawaii's kids experience it everywhere:
Parents sacrifice for "a perfect place out there."
After all is said and done,
Imagine what kids' become
Once they're three score years and ten?

Few parents have the chance to know,
Surmise what offspring's lives could show.

The following describes my visit to a former men's
college that is now coeducational as mostly all are. A

group of alums invited me to their 50th reunion dinner. I'm certain all lived meritoriously and brought pride to their parents as they rose to positions they now hold. They're referred as "boys" in this narrative because it's what they were when first knowing each other.

Some class members walked in appearing a bit stiff and unbending. Remarkably soon, without even one sip of a cocktail, each relaxed quickly among his fellows. It was as if they'd stepped back in time.

Has there any old fellow got mixed with the boys?
If there has, take him out without making a noise.
Hang the almanacs and the catalog's spite.
Old Time is a liar. We're twenty tonight.

An enthusiastic buzz grew, bartenders became busy, laughter rose . . . *The Gang's All Here!* I imagined them thinking:

We're twenty! We're twenty! Who says we are more?
He's tipsy—young jackass. Show him the door.
Gray temples at twenty? Yes! White if you please.
Where the snowflakes fall thickest, there's nothing can freeze.

Men's appearances change when hairlines go, cheeks grow, and pounds pile on. These fellows are experiencing a change in reverse! Some arrived looking somewhat stuffy—disguised as judges, doctors, and investment counselors. Deep, resonant voices came from caverns within their bodies from living those roles.

Now they're animated! Voices rise an octave, becoming head tones. Everyone speaks rapidly, excitedly:

We've a trick, we young fellows,
You may have been told,
Of talking in public as if we were old:

That boy we call 'Doctor' and
This we call 'Judge'
It's a neat little fiction—
Of course it's all fudge.

I walked over to a gentle-looking couple sipping iced tea. They'd operated the family's industrial embroidery business. Grandfather came from Switzerland where he'd learned the craft.

Grandfather taught his son, and his son taught his son—the 72-year-old with whom I'm talking. A slight, enthusiastic freshman when I was a senior, now he's disguised as an elderly man.

Their company made soldiers' military patches. This couple worked in the factory alongside employees.

They'd been through hard times: It was so difficult to find dedicated workers. He persevered, trusting in his Christian faith.

Seeing exquisite examples of sewing while on a church mission in Cambodia, he invited some of the sewing families to work with him.

He provided transportation, housing, and language lessons. Then came financial management lessons, then "Americanization" lessons leading to citizenship. Then he introduced investment lessons. He also taught the Bible to anyone who was interested. Business expanded.

During the few minutes we talked, he expressed pride in his employees, told me about workers' bright children and professional careers some engaged in after college. He described a young Ukrainian boy whose father had deserted him. The boy responded to my friend's guidance, and I was told:

"Now he has a good job, investments—and a Mercedes-Benz!"

This quiet, Christian gentleman turned his family's business over to employees. He lives a peaceful life in New York's Catskill Mountains.

"Your Hawaii is known as Paradise," he said. "We, too, enjoy God's wonders, loving every season of the year."

He described feeding deer and wild turkeys around his property in the winter, skating on the family pond, and burning wood in the fireplace from trees grown for that purpose. "I like to split wood," he cheerfully said.

He talked of holidays when first-and second-generation families of many nationalities fill his home:

"Out of respect and affection, we're called 'Auntie' and 'Uncle!'"

You hear that boy laughing?
You think he's all fun,
But the Angels laugh too
At the good he has done.
The children laugh loud
As they troop to his call,
And the poor man who knows him
Laughs loudest of all.

Dinner was served to us in a large room filled with joy. After dessert the Alumni All-Stars Band played swing music and couples came onto the floor. Some were really excellent dancers. The band didn't have to leave; it was memory night, no one would be driving anywhere, dorm rooms were ready.

We're boys, always playing
With tongue or with pen
And I sometimes have asked:

Shall we ever be men?
Shall we always be youthful
And laughing and gay?
'Till the last dear companion
Drops smiling away.

Calendars turn backwards at high school alumni reunion dinners as well, these are so popular in Hawaii.

Gaudeamus Igitur, a universal academic hymn, is about living. Carpe diem—"savor the moments" and recall them in years to come. Some say youth is in the mind:

Gaudeamus Igitur,
Juvenus dum summus:
Let us now in youth rejoice,
None can justly blame us.

Poetry describing a college reunion may have originated with Oliver Wendell Holmes' reflections on his 50th Harvard College reunion. I heard an old-timer recite such lines at a dinner party many years ago, retained what I could, and imagined the rest. JAR.

Plantations

Donald Dias, former police detective, is paralyzed and wheelchair-bound from a trauma. He keeps in touch with high school classmates and is still one of our most talkative.

We visit him periodically in his one-level house in Ewa Beach. Everyone brings food, we "talk story."

Donald and Twila Dias attend outings such as our class's "All-you-can eat Chinese lunches" in Aiea. Some classmates living on other islands are there. All have reached the mellow time when keeping in touch feels real good.

Donald doesn't want to be left out of anything. He reminds us: "My chair rolls, you know."

So does his ready mind.

He talked. I recorded.

14.

Have Brain, Will Travel

Donald Dias said: "People ask me about growing up on a plantation in Aiea, the area where I've lived all my life. Memory causes me to slip into Pidgin—Aiea's one-time universal language, due to ethnic makeup of workers assigned there. Pidgin English identifies me with that culture.

"But knowing you for over 60 years, I'll avoid reverting. Turn on your tape recorder, and we'll roll."

"Just say what's on your mind," I told him.

Here we go.

* * *

Arriving in 1932, I've lived in Ewa ever since—except for a war excursion in Korea. I've watched this region change from endless scenic cane fields into miles and miles of tract housing. The new look epitomizes the Contemporary American Dream, I guess.

We moved here after a mayor was voted out; father lost his city job and was replaced—political spoils system at work. His new plantation job included use of a little house, at no cost, in the Waimalu pump area, where present-day Pearlridge Shopping Center is. We looked down on an artesian system coming from the ground, now Sumida's Watercress Farm. Water pumped from there irrigated Aiea's sugarcane fields.

My father drove a big White flatbed truck outfitted with a cage and benches. At about 4:30 in the morning he picked up workers assigned to irrigate the fields. He returned to the village to drive their children to area schools—Aiea, Waimalu, Pearl City, and Halawa Elementary. Then he picked up elderly people and took them to their medical appointments at Aiea Hospital. In the afternoon he returned people to where they'd boarded the truck.

On Saturdays, he took plantation children to weekend activities—Hi-Y and YMCA clubs, competitive sports activities with children from other plantations in Ewa, Waipahu, Waialua, Wahiawa, Haleiwa, and Kahuku. Plantation community kids competed in basketball, baseball, and barefoot football. Country schools didn't have high school sports, as did Honolulu's schools.

Our camp consisted of four homes and one pump house. Aiea Hospital was nearby. Farther up was another camp, above what is now Pearl Country Club.

After about a year, we moved to New Mill Camp, adjacent to the sugar mills. Our growing family needed more room; the plantation helped us to move everything. Changing surroundings, meeting new people, not being so isolated seemed entertaining to us kids. A dormitory for single men was across the road—they had their own bedrooms, a furo (outdoor bath), and ate communal style in a cafeteria. Pidgin and sign language were the only ways for us to mutually communicate. Kids are inquisitive, you know.

Housing was always rent-free, part of the benefits of a plantation job.

A year later, in 1937, we moved above New Mill Camp where the plantation built ten new homes. The Big Five, controllers of plantations, ordered lumber in logs in the State of Washington; these were connected together and floated behind ships. Salt water treated the lumber and got rid of bugs.

Each plantation had its own lumber mill where lumber was cut to size for home building. Honolulu Iron Works supplied the corrugated metal roofs, a plantation-housing trademark. When traveling through the Islands, if you spotted a corrugated metal roof, you knew a plantation was nearby.

From our new house we looked straight into Battleship Row in Pearl Harbor. You realize what we saw down there three years later on December 7, 1941. . . .

In 1948 the plantation notified some of the residents, including my father, that they would be allowed to buy their home. Those not receiving this notice had to move within thirty days. That is one example of why it paid to stay on management's good side.

In 1949 the ILWU called a dock strike and halted outgoing shipments of all plantations' products. That gave Honolulu Plantation's owners the excuse to pull the plug—to shut down. There wasn't much the unions could do. They squawked loudly and threatened a lot of things. But *pau hana*—it was over.

* * *

Donald has what we used to call "His Portuguese Magic"—a winning smile. He beamed it on me, although his head was quivering a bit. "I need to take a break," he said. May I pick up later?"

"Absolutely. Why don't you reflect on things; I'll be back in a week."

Donald again displayed his magic.

15.

Vignettes: Donald Dias

Donald's been recollecting his experiences since our last talk; now he's ready to share them. I turn on my recorder, and into the past his agile mind glides. . . .

* * *

Musicians performed on weekends at the taxi stand beneath the banyan tree by Moanalua Road and Aiea Heights Drive. Aiea's General Store sold almost everything there—life's essential sundries all under one roof.

The store was a large, wide-open space. Merchandise was spread out on the counters, arranged into "departments"—linen, clothing, charcoal stoves, school lunch tins. Workers recited their "bongo" number to the store manager when checking out; he marked down what they owed in a book. On the next payday, workers settled what they could with the store.

Plantations paid workers twice a month, taking the pay out to them in the fields. Many frugal families started businesses with what they saved. They have their own story of realizing free enterprise in Hawaii.

* * *

I commented on what I'd learned at newspapers in Pennyslvania coal regions:

"Hawaiian plantation workers experienced a better system than coal miners did throughout the United States.

"Tennessee Ernie Ford's song 'Sixteen Tons' groans, *I owe my soul to the company store.* That refers to the truck system of debt bondage when workers were paid with nonexchangeable credit vouchers for goods at the company store. It was usually referred to as 'scrip'—not good anywhere else.

"It was impossible for workers to store up cash savings. They usually lived in company-owned dormitories or apartment buildings, and rent was deducted automatically from their pay.

"Strikes by the United Mine Workers and affiliated unions forced an end to such practices."

* * *

Donald described plantation comings and goings.

Factory sounds: a whistle signaling the start and end of work. Trains hauling cane. Rumbling within the mill when the generator started.

The mill was the village's tallest building. Everyone could see raw cane going into the chute, to be washed, ground. It became molasses in the mill and then brown sugar, to be shipped to California for refining.

* * *

Hawaii abounds with success stories about children of field and mill workers. These are Donald's perspectives:

* * *

School was regarded as an important opportunity. We plantation kids dressed respectfully for it—not sloppily in denim work clothes. Boys who attended a Japanese school later in the day changed into black pants and a white shirt. My sister, as did all girls, wore a dress to school.

Unfortunately, I had to put on button-up shorts with matching shirt. It was not quite a Little Lord Fauntleroy outfit, but almost, and just a little *too cute*. Kids dressed like that in the old *Our Gang* comedy films—my button-up matching short pants and pastel shirt—Yech!

Mother bought the outfits from Yat Loy Clothing's downtown at King, Nuuanu, and Liliha Streets. I went to school dressed that way into my ninth grade year.

In the ninth grade I transferred to Central Intermediate in Honolulu. I didn't want to get out of my mother's car the first day she drove me there. I was a spectacle. Everyone laughed, saying, "Look at that boy!"

Already turning into a man, *so cutely "attired."*

I wanted to join other plantation kids who finished ninth grade and went into plantation fields. They wore respectable work clothes. Kids who stopped schooling after junior high did so to help their parents, particularly if younger kids were in the family.

Plantation families encouraged children to continue their education. It was very sad for those who couldn't.

Waipahu High School was far away, so lots of us plantation kids went to city schools: Robert Louis Stevenson and then Roosevelt if you could speak good English. Since English Standard Schools were very selective, most attended McKinley High School. When it opened in the '30s, Farrington became a mecca for plantation kids.

After enduring my short-pants stage at Central Intermediate, I attended Farrington High School. In my junior year I had the opportunity of moving up the hill to Kamehameha where young men appeared in khaki Army uniforms.

World War II was so much with us. It shut school down for six months.

We tended Victory Gardens. Oldest kids went to work in the pineapple fields, others helped in cane fields.

The military took over the entire area where Aiea High School is now located.

I sold the *Honolulu Star-Bulletin* to soldiers up there after finishing my school day.

The Navy hospital on Halawa Heights, "Aiea Hospital," was constructed in 1941 and deactivated in 1949. Throughout World War II it was a stop for wounded soldiers and marines on their way home from the war in the Pacific.

Following the battle for Iwo Jima, February-March 1945, it was filled to overflowing with 5,676 patients.

After the war, West Coast union organizers came up with their own ideas on labor relations in Hawaii—and plantations eroded into a memory.

* * *

Although he's paralyzed from neck to toes, you've experienced some of what Donald Dias' uneroded memory knows.

His optimistic spirit hasn't faded away.

We live within the shadow of his sunshiny smile, and it's nurtured by his wife Twila's indomitable spirit.

16.

Ewa on My Mind: Simon Nasario

Simon Nasario lives in Barstow, California, and answered my call for reminiscences of earlier days. His life in Ewa, Oahu, started in October 1918.

"I am still okay at 90," his e-mail stated. "Maybe you'll think enough of my story to help me publish it." Here it is:

* * *

I grew up on Ewa Sugar Plantation. During my small-kid time we collected scrap iron, old jelly glasses—anything that could be sold.

We picked *kiawe* beans and sold them to farmers for cattle and hog feed.

Doing so caused flesh wounds!

* * *

All of the islands' *kiawe* trees resulted from a *single* tree planted in Honolulu in 1828 by a Catholic priest from a seed brought from Paris. Early rivalry between the first-to-arrive dominant Protestants and encroaching Catholics led to the saying: *That priest planted kiawe so its thorns would prick you like Christ's crucifixion crown.* Did this testify to Catholicism's power to get under one's skin?

Charcoal made from *kiawe* wood imparts a wonderful flavor to meat similar to mesquite's. *Kiawe,* a really useful tree, is not meant for punishment.

This is what Simon says:

* * *

The Ewa Sugar Company produced and bottled soda pop and sold it in plantation stores in clear or brown bottles—depending on the flavor. The bottling plant relied on us kids to collect and turn in the empty bottles to a store for reuse. We were recyclers! The store rewarded us with free soda pop and a doughnut.

We went into sugarcane fields to gather purslane—pig weed, as we called it—used as feed by people raising pigs on the edge of our village.

When old enough, we did "hoe *hana.*" This meant weeding with hoes in the field for 25 cents a day. Those who attended school only had to do this during "vacations."

* * *

Children were hired in the Territory of Hawaii, as in early-twentieth-century U.S. mills, mines, and factories. Union organizer Mother Jones described them as "stooped little things, round-shouldered, pale, and skinny." Hawaii's kids had the benefit of working in fresh air and (hot) sunshine.

* * *

We were up before 4:30 a.m. to catch the work train.

It dropped us off at a gathering place in the fields where we reported to our *luna*—the foreman. He assigned us to the place to work.

We started hoeing at 6:00 a.m., then had a 15-minute break for breakfast. At 12:00—on the dot—we had a half an hour to eat the lunch we'd packed with us. Then back to hoe *hana* until 4:30. We'd ride the train to an unloading station near home. We were released at 4 p.m. on Saturdays.

We were awarded a bonus for working the maximum days a month and were paid once a month, depending "on the sugar market."

* * *

The "Big Five" began as "Sugar Factors"—financiers to cash-short early-day sugar growers who sometimes had trouble meeting payroll. "Credit" at the plantation store helped keep the sugar community afloat when cash flow was slow.

Some plantations failed, and over time, factors, e.g., the "Big Five," owned the agriculture industry.

* * *

We worked at the foreman's whim. If he wanted us to go home early, he'd shout:

"Eh, *huki pau!*"

This meant, once we finished an area where we were working, we could go home. We'd really put on the steam—like an army marching in double time—to finish the field we were weeding.

May Day was a big holiday. So was the 4th of July. The plantation [hierarchy] transported us to the beach and gave us soda pop and a hot dog. We brought our ethnic foods, too.

All of us plantation families had a grand-old picnic. We were treated to fireworks during the evening.

The plantation had a Christmas party for us in one of the warehouses. Kids put on a play, everyone sang songs—and Santa Claus arrived!

Santa gave all kids a gift, the favorite being a bag of candy, fruit, and nuts.

* * *

Simon Nasario finishes with

"Plantation life's good times are what I remember best."

17.

Tying Up the Devil

Former cowboy David Kuana Lyman became an early-twentieth-century schoolteacher and principal in Kohala on the Big Island. During evenings he rode his horse to plantation camps to teach laborers to read. Being a "Salvationist," he supplied Bibles as textbooks.

An agitator in one camp victimized fellow Filipinos—cheating them in gambling, putting them in debt, and practicing usury. Not wanting outside influence in "his domain," he made plans for Lyman's next visit.

Men waited apprehensively as their teacher rode in, joyfully calling out:

"A-l-o-h-a! Let us read the Lord's words!"

Screaming ferociously, the agitator appeared from behind the barracks, twirling a bolo in each hand. He was going to use these large sugarcane-hacking knives to knock Lyman from his horse.

Lyman halted his horse, uncoiled the rope attached to his saddle, twirled it around his head, lassoed the troublemaker, and twisted the rope around his saddle horn.

He kicked his heels into the horse's belly and it trotted forward. The agitator fell on his stomach, dropping the bolos.

Lyman yelled, "Whoa!" The horse stopped and defecated—almost on cue.

"Giddy-up," Lyman urged. The horse dragged the roped offender face first, back and forth through the manure.

Lyman tied the shocked, dazed, shit-faced villain to a fence.

Quietly, workers went into their barracks and opened their Bibles. They would read John 14, a chapter spoken in the Passover chamber: *In my Father's house are many mansions. I go to prepare a place for you.* Lyman discussed loving friends because of their "character."

During the night the Devil untied himself.

Never again was he seen in the camp. Now debt-free, talked into reading instead of gambling, workers sent money to families in the Philippines.

Grandpa wrote daily on margins of his six-inch-thick Study Bible.

It became a logbook of Hawaiian cowboy wisdom and scriptural interpretation.

Mine, now, it is a reservoir from which I drink deeply.

Ranching

British sea captain George Vancouver brought several head of cattle to King Kamehameha in 1794.

Their novelty soon wore off. Cattle wreaked havoc throughout the countryside.

John Parker, a sailor who had jumped ship and settled in the Islands, received permission from Kamehameha to capture the wild cattle and develop a beef industry.

This will bring you up to date.

Soot Bredhoff.

18.

Riders on the Black Lava

On Hawaii's movie screens, Tom Mix, Gene Autry, and Roy Rogers pictured what Western lore novelist Zane Grey popularized in *Riders of the Purple Sage* (1912).

Carl "Soot" Bredhoff and Manoa-area elementary school buddies brought it all to life.

Being the darkest in his gang—his mother was part-Hawaiian—Carl was designated "The Red Man" in Cowboys and Indians games. He used charcoal to cover his face and body with "war paint" so intense, so black-and-white-movie realistic that the Manoa cowboys called him "Soot."

Bredhoff explains:

"I waved my wooden tomahawk fiercely, my blood-curdling shrieks made sleeping dogs bark. I never scalped anyone, but I did jerk cowboys' blonde hair firmly so they'd remember being had!"

That monicker "Soot" stuck with Carl Bredhoff, even after he became a professional cowboy on Hawaii's lava rock ranges.

Being a Hawaiian cowboy was an adventuresome and manly vocation. Tom Mix appeared in hundreds of cowboy films between 1910 and 1936 and had an enthusiastic audience in "cowboy-crazy" Hawaii.

Hawaii's Ikua Purdy became "The World Champion Cowboy" in Cheyenne, Wyoming, during a 1908 rodeo. Archie Kaaua took third place, and Jack Low's flamboyancy thrilled the crowds. The three-man Island team used Wyoming scrub horses no one else wanted and practiced on them in a deep river to develop affinity between horse and rider.

Grandpa David Kuaana Lyman, a Kohala cowboy and Purdy's friend, explained:

"Horses are real responsive when you speak to them in Hawaiian." He taught me to toss a horsehide leather rope and snap a bullwhip so sharply that it sounded like a pistol shot!

Purdy's cachet carried: Being a cowboy in Hawaii made you special—even if you could only wiggle your hips and pretend you were on a bucking horse while acting out the popular hula song, "Hawaiian Cowboy," composed to honor Purdy, Kaaua, and Low.

Some of Mix's old flicks were played so often they became "flickie"; Carl's father fixed 'em. Arriving in 1912 from Oakland, California, Carl Sr. and his dad, Henry Bredhoff, owned the Hawaii Film Supply company.

Well-known photographers Tom and Jack Matsumoto worked out of that store. It had a darkroom, too. The Bredhoffs sold motion picture equipment to theater owners.

Punahou trackman Soot outran other teams' Red Raiders, Warriors, Saints, Rough Riders, and Micks. Taking his stamina to Colorado State (Colorado A&M in those days), he played halfback both ways —offense and defense—during the time its football team scheduled Colorado University and Arizona University.

Like other young islanders of his era, Soot worked summers at Del Monte Cannery and California Packing Co. He joined Jimmy Greenwell on "The Kill Floor" in Hawaiian Meat Company's slaughterhouse in summers 1956 and '57.

Returning home with a degree in animal husbandry, Soot did military basic training at Schofield Barracks, then spent six and a half years in the Army Reserve—de rigueur at that point in American history.

Maybe it resulted from movies he saw, having lived near a dairy, or from the excitement of athleticism—Soot was determined to be an outdoorsman.

Most local jobs in those days, from keeping track of money to cutting cane and pineapples, involved Big Five companies, ranching included.

"I talked with folks associated with the Hawaiian Sugar Planters Association," Soot says. "They couldn't woo me into sugar, engineering, or farming."

This was before Willie Nelson's 1978 song warned, *Mama's don't let your sons grow up to be cowboys*. Having parental approval, Soot lived his dream in Hawaii's oldest, most prestigious, and most macho outdoor vocation.

Cattle came to Hawaii in 1794 as a gift to Kamehameha I from Captain Vancouver. John Parker, a New England sailor, befriended the king and became a rancher—yep, *that* Parker Ranch, one of America's largest and oldest!

By the early 1940s, Hawaii ranching had a colorful international cachet through the works of best-selling novelist Armine von Tempski (her nom de plume), daughter of ranch manager Louis von Tempsky. She described Hawaiian cowboy life on Haleakala Ranch, managed by her father. *Born in Paradise* is her girlhood story; she wrote Island-based *Pam's Paradise Ranch* and *Bright Spurs* among others.

Soot said, "I had a job interview with Franny Morgan at Kualoa Ranch, on Oahu. He didn't ask about my college credentials—just wanted to see me ride a horse."

The ride made him a *paniolo,* the Hawaiian word for cowboy, also called *paniolo pipi.* "*Pipi*" means cattle; a variation, "*bipi,*" designates beef cattle. (*Paniola* is a late variation of *paniolo.*)

Morgan managed good-quality purebred *bipi*— Herefords, Angus. They were fed corn, small grains, alfalfa, guinea grass, and pineapple silage.

To be realistic about ranching, you need to forget authors' words and film producers' imagery. Ranching— especially in rocky Hawaii—is *just plain hard work.*

Ranchers live their profession 24 hours a day, seven days a week. There are no holidays; they must constantly feed animals or move them to grazing areas, make certain they have water in the event of droughts, and ensure their safety in open fields. During droughts, cowboys may burn the needles from *panini*—prickly pear cactus plants—and chop them down so cattle can chew the fruit for moisture.

Ranches are largely on what was or still is lava.

"A'a"—the sharp, dry, rough black lava—is a Hawaiian synonym for "fury." It quickly rips shoe soles. Grazing grass may grow in coves planted by cowboys—in this regard cowboys are farmers. Lava turns into soil—eventually. In some places, forests are so thick that a horse and rider have to move slowly while cattle bull on.

Cowboys catch cattle running wild, fix fences, shoe horses, train them, and drive cattle herds.

Soot explains, "On a drive, we work the cattle gently, picking out the leaders, directing them, letting them think they're the boss."

Soot ranched on Oahu, Maui, and Hawaii and spent time in lots of lava country, especially when working for C. Brewer and Kahuku Ranch in Ka'u. Miles of lava lead to the sea.

Judith Pillman, a teacher from Ka'u High School in Pahala, lived in a little cottage on the edge of a spring that rose and fell with the sea tide. Late one night, a herd of cattle crossed the spring to investigate her yard and became stranded when the tide came in.

Judith awoke to see their huge, curious heads looking in the window at her. They paid no attention when she tried to shoo them away. Judith called the ranch for help. Soot arrived—not on a Tom Mix-type of white horse, but in a light-colored jeep.

If this story were portrayed as an old-time cowboy movie, at this phase the sun would set slowly on the screen as music rises dramatically.

That would evoke a happy ending, when Soot meets his future wife.

They've been married for 42 years.
Yippie kai aie-ay!

Soot Bredhoff and Bipi.

19.

Premier Grass-Fed Beef

My periodic visits to a Midwest client included dinner at the Omaha Prime Restaurant in the Old Market District. The maitre d'hotel would proudly state, "Our prime steak is the finest in the world. We serve only Nebraska corn-fed beef."

I'd be treated to a porterhouse, medium-rare.

Celebrating my return to the Big Island after a long absence, I joined schoolmates in Daniel Thiebaut's Restaurant in Waimea.

Seeing "Local ranch grass-fed steaks" on the menu, I quipped: "Remember when only kamaaina were tough enough to eat local beef?"

My friends stared patronizingly. Adjusting behavior to fit with the elegant surroundings, I quickly, quietly studied the elaborate menu.

I ordered a New York cut of the Kamuela beef, grilled medium-rare over *kiawe* coals, and asked for a side dish of Kahua Ranch lettuce with field greens from the same farm, dressed with Kona herbs. The waiter nodded approvingly. I bought two fine bottles of wine for the table. Schoolmates forgot about my sarcasm.

Leaner and redder than Nebraska's finest, the tender steak's flavor was every bit as good, *if not better.* I later repeated the experience with a Maui grass-fed beef porterhouse steak at Kaimuki's 3660 On the Rise restaurant. Equally impressive!

Wanting to know about Hawaii's grass-fed beef's evolution, I talked with Carl "Soot" Bredhoff; he's spent about a half century as an island rancher.

Soot used a Charles Dickens' twist to summarize Hawaii's ranching evolution: *From the best of times, into the worst of times.*

He added, "We're experiencing the new age of wisdom."

Good Times

During post–World War II, America's meat business became industrialized—to increase production, take costs away from the farmer, and boost volume.

In Hawaii, calves weaned from their mothers at six months were sent to mainland feedlots where they gorged themselves to bulk up.

Shipping grain to Hawaii to feed cattle was more expensive than the cost of shipping 500-pound calves to mainland feedlots. There, a well-honed fattening process, with lots of corn, soy, and synthetic FDA-approved hormones, made beef plentiful for consumers and profitable for processors.

Hawaii's grocers and restaurateurs imported practically all beef consumed by local residents and visitors. Consumers paid top dollar, as demand for beef was high. Feedlot beef had the taste and uniformity Americans came to expect.

Worst Times

Prices supporting Hawaii's ranches dropped when New Zealand entered the U.S. market in the 1980s. Memories of good-old ranching days faded as New Zealand beef flooded the market.

Wiser Times

Ranchers diversified; some added "tourism," as did Monty Richards of Kahua Ranch. He raises Angus, Herefords, Charolais, and Wagyu cattle (the latter are what Japanese use for Kobe beef). His ranch entertains guests, grows tomatoes hydroponically, and Richards raises greens for restaurants and consumers. Kahua Ranch operations are powered by wind and solar energy.

Small ranchers' operations sprang up after Hamakua Coast sugar mills closed in the mid-1990s. Instead of shipping their calves to the mainland, ranchers hung on and raised grass-fed meat as trends in that direction evolved.

In "The Grass-Fed Revolution" (January 11, 2006), *Time* magazine reported the following: "Grass is a low-starch, high-protein fibrous food, in contrast to carbohydrate-rich, low-fiber corn and soybeans. When animals are 100% grass-fed, their meat is not only lower in saturated fats, but is also slightly higher in omega-3 fatty acids which studies indicate may help prevent heart disease and bolster the immune system."

Time also stated, "Data suggest grass-fed beef may prevent breast cancer, diabetes, and other ailments. It is higher than grain-finished meat in vitamin A and vitamin E, two antioxidants thought to boost resistance to disease."

Kulana Foods on Hawai'i island buys grass-fed cattle from local ranchers, as does North Shore Cattle Company on Oahu and Maui Cattle Company on the Valley Isle. Processed locally, Hawaii's grass-fed beef is marketed as premium Big Island meat on the mainland, as well as throughout Hawaii.

Several mainland companies produce natural beef without hormones and antibiotics. Country Natural Beef is supplied by several of our local ranches, members of the Hawaii Cattle Producer's Cooperative. Their beef is sold in Whole Food stores.

Hawaii's calves are shipped to the mainland, pastured on grass, then sent to a feedlot where they're fed a special ration. Mainland companies such as Laura's Lean Beef and Maverick Ranch are supplied with Hawaii cattle.

Hawaii's grass-fed cattle graze in open pastures year-round on a diet of grass and legumes. They remain in local pastures 15 to 18 months longer than cows sent to feedlots. They don't grow as big as feedlot cattle. Breeding stock staying in Hawaii eventually is used in hamburger or cheaper cuts like teriyaki and stew meat.

Alan Wong's is one of the Honolulu fine restaurants to feature premium-quality Big Island grass-fed steaks; Maui grass-fed beef is "seasonally available" at 3660 On the Rise. Town, a Kaimuki restaurant, proudly features a wide selection of Island-raised grass-fed beef.

According to Ed Kenny, Town's owner, "Our beef comes from a handful of sources. Our longest supplier of pasture-raised beef and only cattle ranch on Oahu is North Shore Cattle Company. It is a small operation owned and operated by the Lum family in Waialua, Oahu. We also have obtained pasture-raised beef from Puu o Hoku Ranch on the east end of Molokai."

Kenney explains, "Our grass-fed strip loin comes from a cooperative of cattle ranches on the Big Island that process and distribute their beef through Kulana Foods. Each ranch has signed an affidavit outlining the "intensive grazing" methods they must practice in order to be sold through Kulana. Newest addition to the market is Kuahiwi Ranch in Ka'u on Hawaii island; it offers a grain supplement for the last 90 days before slaughter."

"Nearly a million acres of Hawaiian land is ranched and held together by a fierce sense of place," Bredhoff says. The Hawaii Cattlemen's Council, headed by rancher Jim Greenwell, wrestles with legislation representing an economic threat to the livestock and grazing industry. Politicians are tantalized by thoughts of "added value from ranging land" through higher taxes from real estate development, including "gentlemen farms."

Bredhoff explains, "Ranchers protect the land as economic conditions permit. We plant native species and restore wetlands on unused land. We restore wildlife habitats for endangered and threatened species. We reduce soil erosion, protect streams; doing this helps coral reefs grow.

"Once ranch land is gone, it is lost forever. We grow food and strive to preserve the life of the land. That's a throwback to the days of cowboy movie heroes wearing white cowboy hats.

Sumida Watercress Farm.

20.

Song and Dance

Here's a country dance with steps and kicks sung to the tune of "Cotton-Eyed Joe."

Civil War–era folk singers used music like "Cotton-Eyed Joe" for singsong comments on life during *Pre-Reconstruction Days*. These words are about Hawaii's *Construction Phases*.

As growers of food we also strive
To keep Hawaiian land's life alive.
Land developers are our threatening force;
Legislators want high revenues—of course.

Housing, resorts, estates increase land value,
Can tax more for people than plants or cattle.
Productive land once gone is lost forever:
Honest work exchanged by those who act clever.

As growers of food we also strive
To keep Hawaiian lands' life alive.

Hawaii's leaders won't say, "That's enough;"
Easy-becomed politicians aren't that tough,
Invite: "Visit, stay, congest, help us grow,
Fecundity is big-time here, don't you know?"

"Love of Aina" now means having some action,
"Expand, build, make us rich" is the reaction,
Real estate marketers turnover and flip.
Investors arrive, can do it fast—one trip.

Avoid groundwork; opt for the pie-in-sky schemes,
Arising cities, rail, comprise the new dreams.

As growers of food we also strive
To keep Hawaiian lands' life alive.

One-party legislators smile, say "We're Friends,
Just do paperwork and amends and amends.
Aunt Sally here, Uncle Solly there know all,
For a good deal make sure they're ones who you call.
Hey, look at your watch. Time now for some *kaukau!*
Eat with my union pals: they've strength and know-how.

As growers of food we also strive
To keep Hawaiian lands' life alive.

Once schmoozing ends, and you commit, things get tough.
Delays, to please so many, never enough.

"E.A.S? No worry 'til the frowns come by,
Just give-um, schmooze, why not chance a good try?

As growers of food we also strive
To keep Hawaiian lands' life alive.

These Cowboy verses from Paniolo Soot
Describe local ranchers' story all through it:
"Been a Hawaiian Cowboy all of my life,
Made a lava-field rescue and met my wife.
Love of land and tradition deserves to stay:
Ranching and Ag—Vital to Hawai'i Nei!"

Land and animal husbandry is their work
Seven-day care of cattle they never shirk.

"What we do for others should matter to you,
Growing grass-fed beef good for health and to chew.
Ours is not industrial food, it's raised slow,
This premium beef, the best kind you will know,
High protein, low starch, not saturated fat.
Seeking to preserve natural habitat.
Help native plants grow, wetlands where they're at.

"Valuable birds need old-time precipices,
Restore habitats for endangered species,
Reducing soil erosion, protecting streams—
So the coral reefs will grow, being kept clean!"

As growers of food we also do strive
To keep Hawaiian ocean life alive.

Watercress, tangy, tasty, crispy to chew,
Put in soups or eat fresh 'cause it's good for you,
By Aiea's main highway is where it thrives,
Stream and Sumida's workers, keep it alive.

Lesser prevents Pearlridge mall encroachment,
Keeps oasis: brings life and enjoyment.
See empty box stores at the parking lot?
Rich soil, water, food crops grew on that spot!

Three generation-Sumida's plants grow,
Will high-flying developers cause woe?
Big bucks from the Continent can make friends,
High leases more taxes: Tempting amends.

As growers of food we also strive
To keep Hawaiian land's life alive.

Politicians change our way of life,
One-party dominance avoids all strife.
High-rises, highways, rails to Fat City,
Favors help legislators sit pretty.

Land developers are a threat'ning force:
Legislate for high revenue, of course.
"Ecology Tourism," not our game,
Beaches, shops, good weather—elsewhere's the
same.

Land use restrictions fall between the crack,
One-time public beach rules are out of whack.
Some rich folks do whatever they Dam please,

Plow, cover-up, Kapu: Paradise thieves.

As growers of food we also strive
To keep Hawaiian land's life alive

Kamehameha Schools

Boys attended a military-boarding school teaching manual labor and how to conform. No lawyers sued for client entrance.

These were all part of students' daily norms:
Clean the classrooms, common areas in dorms.
Scrub the toilets also the showers—
Missed spots will bring detention hours.
Shine all the windows, wax the floors
Earn positive inspection scores.
Trash must be gleaned!
Dust specks not seen!
Trim brush, mow grass;
Walk on hard paths.

Students building the football field
Work there by demerits—not zeal.
Cooks are kitchens' only paid employees;
Students do all else because they are "free."

Peel, serve, be polite as a waiter;
From dishes and pots scrub off all flavor.

Constant inspection to spot shirkers
Football field always needs new workers.
Hair can't touch your ear;
Shoes shine brightly clear.
"Girls' experience in work sharing,
Makes them more creative and caring."
Girls' principal uses euphemisms;
The school is known as staunchly Christian.

Boys all have "shop" for at least two years—
Take home a monkey pod lamp made here.
Shops prepare us to meet job demands:
Auto, machine, electric work hands.
The co-ed print shop staff is not meek:
Publishing school newspaper every week.

Senior cottage girls learn marriage isn't "heaven":
Plan meals, cook, do baby care 24/7.
Girls all sew their own graduation gown;
"Finishing School refinement is renown."

These represent only slices few—
There were academic classes, too.
But all who loved hard work
Had a good time there!

21.

Not So Bad Being Me

Along with experiencing the Depression, Wars, and Hawaii's lost economic engine, our generation gained a head start on tomorrow.

I joined new brothers in a cloistered military boarding school on Kapalama Heights. We came from all islands—mostly within the boondocks.

Boys lived there up to seven years before World War II, beginning with seventh grade; some experienced low- and high-eleventh grades. Kamehameha schoolboys received on-the-job training in Honolulu, the reason for two eleventh-grade years.

We were given a pass to visit Honolulu on Saturday, provided our manual labor met performance standards.

These experiences would later lead me to comparing beautiful Honolulu to hospitable Charleston, South Carolina, because of that southern city's gracious historic buildings, downtown benches, and its flowering urban gardens.

When restless white men arrived, the ground on which Honolulu stands was a dry, dusty plain. They filled the swamps, dredged new land from the sea, built the harbor and the impressive office buildings comprising Honolulu's little Wall Street that are clustered at Fort and Merchant Streets.

The whites drove tunnels into Oahu's mountains to capture underground waters, making Honolulu a city of flowering trees.

The Big Five, a white businessmen network, created a paternalistic, almost feudal pastoral realm. They called it "Paradise of the Pacific."

My brothers and our sisters at Kamehameha School for Girls graduated as industrious men and women.

The day after Pearl Harbor, Hawaii became a beehive in a state of siege, with all civil rights ignored by the military autocracy.

Following V-J Day (Victory-over-Japan Day), islanders performed a near miracle in removing the shambles of barbed wire on beaches, mountains of military junk, and miles of drab barracks.

Union organizers soon heaved paternalism out the window, adopted collective bargaining, and hiked wages to near-mainland standards. The pendulum of power swung from big employers to flushed union leaders supporting the new, powerful Democratic machine.

The pendulum swung so far back that agricultural operations in Hawaii were no longer competitive with low-cost labor elsewhere. Hawaii's economic engine slowed and eventually stopped—sugar and pineapple could be grown far cheaper in another place.

"Tourism" was ballyhooed by new waves of businessmen—old-timers worried, would "tourism" be enough?

"I just growed," Topsy said in the movie *Gone with the Wind*. Same thing happened here. Developers poured in. Hawaii began resembling frenetic overbuilt Hong Kong, not preservation-perfect Charleston.

Big Democrats, taking over from the Big Five, controlled what was happening. The outcome demonstrates their vision and aestheticism.

Freedom of opportunity had seemed a myth to Hawaii's population majority: It's why so many favored statehood.

Statehood Day celebrations swept through the Islands in 1959. Communities lit bonfires, neighborhoods held impromptu dances, cars blared horns, folks walked the streets with broad grins and greetings.

Orientals, who arrived here to work in plantations and sent sons to war in the American Army, viewed themselves as full-fledged Americans. Both political parties were together in the quest for Hawaiian statehood. Hawaii's media were in full support as well. Opposition voices were silent.

Hawaiians had been silent as well on the subject of land. *The Indices of Awards Made by the Board of Commissioners to Quiet Land Titles in the Hawaiian Islands* (1840) states, "This is a legacy to acquire real estate in Fee Simple on all of the islands." Thousands of Hawaiian surnames are listed for awards ranging from 4 to 7,000 acres. What happened to this land? Was it *really* stolen? (I'm studying and tracking, and may sometime comment.)

Less than a decade after statehood, the modern Native Hawaiian Sovereignty movement emerged as a cause celebre among youthful advocates. Now activists question things we never would. (We're *makule* [old] and have perspectives differing from outspoken *moopuna* positions.)

> *Young men,**
> *Young men,*
> *What do the young men want?*
> *Young men want everything that they see.*
> *The only thing that young men don't want*
> *Is ever to grow old like me.*
>
> *That's the way we were once:*
> *Is it so hard to remember?*
> *But now is not so bad,*
> *In fact, it's rather nice;*
> *For some things don't come your way*
> *Until it's December!*
>
> *So dream on young men,*
> *Dream and follow your dreams.*
> *And some day you'll learn*
> *It's not so bad becoming someone like me.*

*"*Men*" applies as a collective noun for "mankind"—e.g., the human race. Poesy pertains to kane *and* wahine.

22.

Forbidden Culture

This headline describes policies in Hawaiian and American Indian Schools. Hard to believe in America's enlightened twenty-first century, wouldn't you say?

People and things called "Hawaiian" now have cachet. The ubiquitous Hawaiian hula may have more enthusiasts in Japan than "The Twist" ever had in America!

Realizing I'm dating myself by conjuring Chubby Checker, I'll unfold this dated story on how things were.

Kamehameha School for Boys was once the main hope for young Hawaiians who didn't have a chance in life. It had a social as well as economic "mission" handed down from the missionaries. During the late 1940s, 5 percent of its boys were pure Hawaiian, 60 percent were seven-eighths to half Hawaiian, and most came from meager circumstances.

Trustees interpreted Princess Pauahi's will as welcoming to youngsters who might otherwise never achieve their potential.

School recruiters visited all islands. During my time, the Girls School admitted a student from Niihau, able to speak only Hawaiian, the forbidden language. Being very bright, she quickly acquired English and thrived—she returned to Niihau as a teacher, using Hawaiian where it wasn't forbidden.

Many of us came from poor and broken homes—orphanages in several cases—most wouldn't qualify for Hawaii's English Standard Schools because of language skills. Nothing "Hawaiian" could be voiced on campus, except when singing "The Doxology" before dinner or when performing in the yearly song contest. We sang in English only during wartime morale-building evening assemblies.

We wore bland khaki uniforms and blue work clothes. Dancing the hula got you kicked out of school—it happened to Nona Beamer in 1941. Her *tutu* convinced trustees it was all a horrible mistake, and she was readmitted on probation.

Samoans from "way down there" visited in 1949; briefly, barriers went down. Their language sounded Hawaiian except for consonants not in our language. Our word "aloha," for instance, was their word *"talofa."*

That's because New England Protestant missionaries changed our language that once was similar to what's spoken in Tahiti and Samoa. For example, Kamehameha originally was known as "Tamehameha."

Missionaries concocted a written language, simplifying it by using all vowels and just seven consonants: h, k, l, m, n, p, w; a consonant is followed by a vowel.

We listened raptly to sounds flowing from their mouths. Young men wore lavalavas—skirts wrapped around their waists to just below their knees; young women's garb covered most of their upper bodies as well.

During their last night on campus, Samoans presented an elaborate two-hour program in the school auditorium. Kamehameha Schools had never hosted anything like it: *aboriginal dancing in the school auditorium!*

Samoan dancing was fast and graceful, Tahitian dancing was presto speed—extremely fast and vigorous. Oh my, how they shook and wiggled their *okole!*

For weeks after, students imitated the Samoans, feeling they could get away with it. If questioned, we'd whine: "We aren't dancing the forbidden Hawaiian hula or speaking Hawaiian."

I practiced until I could make a loud sound by briskly bringing my right arm straight down so it slapped against lateral muscles. That's how it was done in a Samoan dance: *Snap, crackle, pop!* I did it at the starting line in a track meet and the nervous Punahou guy almost made a false start.

Senior girls signed pictures in yearbooks using Samoan phrases they'd picked up—*"Talofa"* or *"Fai fai le mu"*—take it easy. Even though it was close to being Hawaiian, they couldn't be punished because they wrote in Samoan.

Some seniors said farewell at the pier when our Samoan "cousins" returned home. We loved their spirit and optimism and culture.

Tears ran down our cheeks as we sang farewell:
Now is the hour, when we must say goodbye;
Soon you will be sailing far across the sea.

That was a thin slice of a forbidden life. Fifteen years later, Booz Allen Hamilton, a mainland consulting firm, delivered a precedent-setting study making a strong case for Kamehameha taking the lead in forwarding Hawaiian culture and heritage.

It directed the Bishop Museum, the University of Hawaii, and the Department of Public Instruction to join this school for Hawaiian boys and girls in answering such questions as:

What are the important values in Hawaiian culture?

Which of these values should be preserved in modern American society?

* * *

You know about Hawaii's culture resurgence.
I wanted to report what led up to it.

23.

Hawaiian Only Sung

Hawaiian language is in the open in the contemporary liberated age. Signs are marked so newcomers can pronounce the words.

Once authorities frowned at the Hawaiian language. The school for Hawaiians allowed it only to be sung in public at each of two annual song contests: One for boys, another for girls.

Credit for the contests goes to Ernest Charles Webster. In 1921, as president of the Kamehameha School for Boys, he initiated a song contest to honor George Alanson Andrus, the school's beloved music teacher who died suddenly. Webster is the grandfather of Marion Lyman-Mersereau, whose poem and a story appear in this volume of *Slices*. Her "squid-eye" mother grew up on the Kamehameha Schools campus.

Webster became dean of the University of Hawaii; Webster Hall on the main campus is named after him.

"Forbidden language" policies were established by school trustees. They were influenced by the Big Five, who in turn were influenced by (their) missionary family beliefs. That's how Hawaii was run.

Curtailing the language was similar to American Indian cultural suppression. The Carlisle Indian School, Pennsylvania, lead school of its type, was a prime example. Students were taught, "Indian ways are bad . . . you must be civilized like the white man."

Jim Thorpe, one of the greatest football players of all time, played for the Carlisle Indians. Its innovative football team was coached by Glenn "Pop" Warner, who added deception, razzle-dazzle, an array of passing, and basically invented the modern game.

Hawaii learned about razzle-dazzle football from Iolani School's coach Father Bray during the time of this story. An ordained Episcopal priest, Father Bray was the friend of Notre Dame Coach Knute Rockne. The Catholic university's coach sent him the super-secret Notre Dame playbook to use at Iolani. Boys on this Hawaii Episcopalian team always puzzled their opponents.

"Being different" is a way to succeed; here's how that was done in a school where Hawaiian was sung.

Song leaders at Kamehameha Schools were each class' most important person. This authority called as many rehearsals as he or she felt were needed and could browbeat anyone for not trying hard enough.

Since song contests were the only times students were permitted to use the Hawaiian language, leaders made certain words were pronounced perfectly. Mary Kawena Pukui, working below campus at the Bishop Museum, was the authority.

By song contest night, students ached to do their best for the person who controlled with the flick of a finger, a glance, a raised eyebrow, an intense look—and who reassured with a smile.

The class winning the contest had bragging rights for a year—or *forever,* as did 18 girls in the class of 1947, directed by vivacious Rowena Vierra.

During early war years, the Girls School was a military hospital. Kamehameha, exclusively for boarding students, dropped its seventh grade early during the war. The girls class of 1947 won song contests during its eighth, ninth, and tenth grades. Under Rowena's direction, they became known as *invincible.*

Girls in the senior class of 1946 had never defeated the class of 1947. They needed to do something dramatic because Vierra-led juniors were virtuosos.

Being in a class that never won a song contest stigmatizes you forever. I know: Our boys' 1949 class lost every song contest, even though exemplary performer Don Ho was our song leader. Sixty years later, we still hear about it.

Anna Eagles, '46, the seniors' song leader, and music teacher Miss Laura Brown made song contest history.

Eagles selected "Nalani," a new contemporary song by Alvin Issacs (later recorded by Alfred Apaka, the sensational-sounding baritone). Finding and choosing the class' prize song was the leader's prerogative; Anna's eagle eyes spotted this one.

Issacs was helping to create a new wave of sensuous modern Hawaiian music. His vocal quartet, the Royal Hawaiian Serenaders, brought him to the attention of Bing Crosby and Hollywood. He was on the cusp of great things when sensitive Eagles sleuthed Issacs' new composition and brought it to campus.

Miss Brown created a sophisticated choral arrangement of "Nalani," giving choral vocal depth to Issacs' tight major and minor harmonies. All was secret. Part of the song contest's mystique involved keeping a class' chosen prize song "undercover."

Miss Brown helped Anna teach classmates to sing like Fred Waring's "Pennsylvanians," a hugely popular mainland choral group with a distinctive style that was . . . well, distinctively Fred Waring!

Words to "Nalani" weren't what you'd expect hearing at the proper Christian missionary-style Kamehameha School for Girls.

Eagles divulged nuances to her classmates—otherwise how could they include such imaginative passion into their singing? The CIA could have learned from these girls about undercover operations. They beamed during rehearsal and pursed their lips nonchalantly when seen on campus.

Judges certainly wouldn't understand what they were hearing. Hawaiian had been outlawed under the mandate of the Territory of Hawaii school system and was almost a dead language.

Schoolmates saw an impish look in Senior Losers' eyes. Confident juniors thought to themselves: "Don't look smug. We're going to beat you again! Snicker, snicker.

The senior class' prize song began with beautiful Hawaiian poetry:

Auhea 'oe Nalani,
Auhea wale 'oe.
He aha no la kau hana,

A liko no 'oe iau.
Which means:
Where are you, Nalani?
Where are you?
What is my desire?
Why, to make you mine!
Intensity increases:
Ke huli nei Nalani,
Ke i'ini nei a'u oe.
Heaha no la kau hana,
A lilo no 'oe i'au.
Interpreted:
Come to me, Nalani,
You are the one I yearn for.
What is my desire?
To make you mine!

Hawaiian words for the next two verses grow with fervor.

Believe me, they do.

Fred Waring and the Pennsylvanians was a combined female and male adult chorus. It changed tempos during a song. Singing rose to a crescendo before suddenly dropping to a whisper. Singers emphasized certain sounds within words. Sounds played on listeners' emotions as Maestro Waring created a cappella magic. That kind of singing brought you to the edge of your seat.

And it's exactly what Anna taught classmates to do.

Being seniors, they were the last to perform on stage. Girls stood in virginal-white dresses with a slightly scooped neckline, dress lines fell to mid-calves, they wore low-heeled, white shoes. Each senior had a deep-red carnation lei around her neck, some may've applied a blush of lipstick—not enough though for school principal Dr. Frederick to notice.

Issacs' contemporary sound and technique, Brown's harmonic effects, and Eagles' total control mesmerized the audience.

At times the girls sang and extended *Na-a-a-a* . . . then, briskly, clipped the two-syllable *la-ni* so it rang and echoed within the 1,000-seat, acoustically perfect, tall, enclosed auditorium.

The song reflected a lover's impatience— comprehended, maybe, by a few older folks in the audience who understood the Hawaiian and wistfully recalled experiences of their own.

Silence hung momentarily when the senior girls finished.

Stunned persons in the auditorium wondered: *Was this Hawaiian music?*

Applause began tentatively at first as awed spectators adjusted tingling ears and emotions.

Such a radical contrast to the four previous classes.

Once hearts were out of their throats, the crowd roared with approval for the creative and courageous senior girls who, obviously, had just won their first song contest!

The judges' decision seemed an afterthought.

The "impossible" happened.

Junior women were devastated, feeling seniors used trickery to beat them. Quickly becoming good sports, they stopped tears from flowing once they realized the 21 senior girls were crying more profusely than they—and simultaneously grinning!

Vierra and her class won the next year's contest, melting the audience with incredibly beautiful singing of the more conventional "Lei Lokelani" ("The Rose Lei"). Words and music to that song were composed in 1921 by school alumnus Charles E. King. He used picturesque— not passionate—words. Harmony was conventional four-part major Kinglike chords; no minor surprises.

I witnessed performances by Eagles' and Vierra's classes in 1946 and by Vierra's class a year later when those 18 seniors won.

After experiencing the seductive whispering sound of "Nalani" from voices of the 21 beautiful, young, impressionable women, I have never been the same.

What I feel is almost a psychic phenomenon. Even over a half century later, when all is quiet, *if I listen carefully,* a lingering whisper wafts high in the tall, old-auditorium.

Auhea 'oe Nalani . . .

24.

'Swipe' Confession

Back in the old days, when I was young,
Good spirits kept us having our fun.
But some boys, when they're sixteen or so,
Want more than just human spirit's glow.

Pranks, hi-jinks were those older guys' stuff,
Thirteen, I agreed—avoid rebuff.

Time for this confession to come through
About the big boys concocting brew.
Goings on in military school—
Statute of limitations are through.

Roommate George, religious Mormon guy,
Won't drink soda for a bubbly high.
He's very tolerant of me, though,
His sixteen siblings made him mellow.

That is why our school stuck me with him—
Innocent of "local bathtub gin."
"Put Kolohe with Kanahele":
Older straight arrow an exemplar.

George's room was the perfect cover;
I could be "conned" as you discover.

Older boys, during a weekend of fun,
Sliced pineapples, let them sit in sun,
Add sugar, active nutrient, and yeast,
Contain in pot, allow space to breathe.

Hide in a box in "our" closet,
Cover with my rumpled clothes and wait.
No one'll note strange smell from our room,
"It's my asthma inhalator fume."

George's smeller is not working well;
Cold, stuffed nose, he doesn't feel too swell.
Don't think he'd notice it anyway;
I develop film there, night and day.

Visitors come in to stir the mess
When George is out—this, too, I confess.
Older guys have a gleam in their eyes,
It's their secret, no one else is wise.

George, a near-Elder and little me—
Us? Who'd suspect a distillery?
Guess the Swipe became excited, too;
Like "the Blow Hole," during one night it "blew!"

Explosion! A yellow geyser high!
Officer of the Day and Big Five
Weren't fooled, they knew what we had alive.

George sighed sadly, sneezed, and blew his nose,
Said, "Look what you did to all our clothes!"
Closeted uniforms all alike
Were now juicy yellow from the Swipe.

Of course, I had to take all the fall,
It happens when you're skinny and small.
My name is "Rath," but I didn't "rat."
It'd mean Big Guys would kill me for *that*
And for the loss of what's in their vat.

Justice came when I returned next fall,
Now, over six-feet, muscles not small.
Whereas, those "Big Guys" seemed to have shrank—
Maybe from Swipe they finally drank.

Since confession now makes this okay,
Here's a warning to help save your day:
If you want to make Hawaiian "Swipe,"
Know it's explosive when nearly ripe!

25.

Teachers' Eternal Influence

I was a 14-year-old boarding student when Mr. Loring Hudson explained how to use the "Inverted Pyramid" and "Who, What, Why," and "When" in news stories.

Reading "The Gripes of Rath," my weekly school newspaper column, the Reverend John Mulholland, chaplain at Kamehameha School for Boys, decided to start me on a magazine writing career. He showed me how a news story or column can be turned into a feature article by adding the element of "How" to the Inverted Pyramid.

"I use that technique for some of my sermons," he confided.

I listened carefully, followed his advice, and for my first article published in a national magazine, submitted with his help, I received fifty dollars. Do you realize its equivalency today? Do you have any idea how much you could buy for that at McInerney's Brothers fine menswear store?

The story was about Joe Pacific's Shoe Repair Shop in downtown Honolulu. "Joe" always gave a free shoeshine to servicemen. The article appeared in *Boot and Shoe Recorder,* top magazine in the footwear field.

At 16 I never looked back: Being published became my being.

That wasn't the end of the Rev. Mulholland's influence on my life. He picked a college for me. His seminary classmate and fellow Presbyterian was Hamilton College's new president, the Rev. Robert Ward McEwen. John Mulholland believed upstate New York would be a dandy place for me to learn how to become a real writer.

Rev. Mulholland was a "career maker" for many youngsters. For example, he encouraged three students from the Class of 1951 to attend his alma mater, Yankton School of Theology, in South Dakota. James P. Merseberg, William H. Kaina, and David K. Kaupu, all who entered the ministry, returned to Hawaii to serve God and extended their own influence.

Being so far away in snow country and attending classes with grizzled World War II veterans terrified me. In my freshman year I was in a selective creative writing seminar; the other five students were impressive upperclassmen. "Having been published," somehow slipped me in the door.

The creative writing seminar cast consisted of senior Don Roescher, who edited the college literary magazine and wrote poetry with meanings escaping me; junior Tom Meehan, who wrote with confidence and enthusiasm and years later won three Tony Awards for *Annie, Hairspray,* and *The Producers;* junior Omar Pound, son of literary genius and Hamilton graduate Ezra Pound, who was translating Persian poetry—then! and senior Jim Collier, a World War II veteran who performed jazz music and published pieces about it. He became a prize-winning author as did five members of his literary family. And there was senior Ray Powers, another World War II vet, optimistic as Meehan and the most outwardly kind of the bunch. Powers became a Catholic priest, was given a new name, and he's written very popular religious books.

When Roescher described some of my early work as "purple," Powers chimed in very kindly, "But it's such a nice shade of purple, Don."

These older men terrified me. Their well-honed and sophisticated language was in such sharp contrast to my Hawaii-based speech. I was kind of *kuaaina* (from the country), let the truth be known.

Responding to my plaintive letter explaining I might be in the wrong place, the Rev. Mulholland answered:

"I have not sentenced you to a Purgatory that will undermine your confidence. Your classmates are older, have read more widely than you, are accustomed to give-and-take discussions."

Commenting on passages in work I'd sent him, he wrote:

"These are good because they come from within you. Keep at it. You won't be left behind."

He shared my letter with Mr. Hudson, who mailed me a book of poetry titled *Kanaka Moon* by Clifford Gessler, a 1920s Hawaii newspaper reporter. The only Island-based poetry I'd read previously was by Don Blanding, known as "Hawaii's Poet Laureate."

Blanding originated "May Day is Lei Day in Hawaii." I thought his couplets, similar to hapa haole songs, were light, frothy, sweet, and nice. They encapsulated white persons' pleasant perspectives. Blanding's cavalier sophistication *wasn't at all what I felt!*

I tried to apply Gessler's tightness and developed personal versions of his dark, moody, and romantic Hawaiian Island imagery. I uncovered my own feelings, even uncovered a touch of my frustrated anger.

We placed our writing in a file at the library for class members to review.

Apparently they liked my metamorphosis; some left anonymous marginal notes such as these:

"Touch of Yeats: resolutely lyrical, sentimental, and subjective." . . . "Misty indolence." . . . "Trace of Fitzgerald's *Rubaiyat*." (How I hoped Omar Pound had written *that!*)

Heady stuff for a terrified 17-year-old!

Generous and nurturing observations from these older men encouraged me to continue describing personal emotions and perspectives and to loosen up and become open.

I mailed examples to my two high school mentors, asking that they share them with Mr. James Vidulich, English teacher and weekly school newspaper adviser. Mr. Vidulich had given me Oscar Wilde's *Salome* as a graduation present.

These three mailed me a box of chocolate-covered macadamia nuts with a card in it reading,

I think you've got it!

I shared those sweet tastes of Hawaii with wise men in the seminar.

My confidence was growing.

Loring Hudson, aged 93, was losing his sight when he traveled from Australia to Honolulu for my class' 45th reunion. He taught at a private school and smilingly confided, "Australian girls read to me."

We were housed in a campus dorm for a week. Hudson's room was across the hall from mine. I accompanied him to wherever he wanted to go, telling him of my writing since he and the Rev. Mulholland started me.

I mailed examples to him in Australia when I was back in New York.

He replied in large handwriting, "Write more poetry" and enclosed *My Kamehameha,* his poem about shared trust and understanding in the school where he inspired so many.

Thinking of those three, I paraphrase William James, nineteenth-century pragmatist:

A teacher's influence is eternal.
One never knows how or where it will end.

26.

High Style at McInerney's Brothers

Attending the eastern men's college of my choice seemed out of the question: I didn't come from a nuclear family—had only a mother. She was out of work, college loans weren't yet invented, and the college of my choice wouldn't offer financial aid because my acceptance was provisional.

It wasn't sure I could do the course work—I'd attended Kamehameha Schools, known mainly for manual arts training.

Summer jobs at Dole Pineapple Cannery and at a Tuna Packing Plant helped me earn enough to pay for my first semester, travel to New York State, and buy some clothes. That was it. The college's provisional acceptance meant I had to prove myself. I was determined to do well and wanted to make a good impression. My choice of clothing wear was important; the adage "clothes make the man" was extant.

Three brothers started McInerney's Brothers, Honolulu's fine menswear store. Edward died in 1923; his younger twins Will and Jim carried the business forward. During my youth, McInerney's was the place where elite did meet. Twins stocked the finest merchandise and provided personalized assistance.

Mother took me there and told Will and Jim of my plans to infiltrate the eastern establishment. She made my undertaking sound like a folk story of Irish peasants moving in on London's high society. I was just seeking upward mobility. Mother was a storyteller. Twins were of Irish stock and storytelling appealed to them.

I had no suitable clothes for the forthcoming cold climate; my leftover Kamehameha School for Boys' wardrobe was khaki cotton military uniforms (CKC) and blue cotton work clothes.

Will and Jim said they were delighted to help me make a favorable impression.

"I don't have much money," I tried to explain.

"Not to worry," Will reassured me.

"You'll get great value," promised Jim.

These two charmers raised my hopes when they said, "We'll make you look so refined they'll realize how lucky they are to have you."

Talking with the two brothers was like communicating with one person. Their minds worked together: When one paused, the other finished his sentence. I couldn't tell Will from Jim.

"The good impression outfits" they selected included an all-purpose, nicely tailored blue blazer.

"Unlike ordinary wool blazers that hang like a bag, this is tapered," one said.

The other displayed charcoal grey flannel pants for my 28-inch waist.

I was receiving tandem service. The other brother brought over Ivy-league style button-down white shirts, an assortment of ties, and dark socks that reached my calves.

"Your existing loafers seem quite serviceable," Jim remarked. Then he asked me to try on Florsheim cardovan wingtip dress shoes. "You'll need to wear these with your suit."

"What suit?" I asked.

"Here it is," Will declared as he led me to a display table.

Out of the side of my eyes, I saw Jim take the shoes to the checkout counter and add Kiwi shoe polish to the shoebox.

"This is for best," Will beamed. He opened a suit bag and began his presentation. Jim joined in. The twins proudly arrayed every element needed to turn me into "a gentleman."

"We suggest you wear this brand new, exclusive and advanced design," Will explained. The Hart-Schaffner Marx double-breasted gray flannel suit had exaggerated shoulders and was tapered at the waist. It was not a "zoot suit," but as Will explained, "It has a modern, rakish memorable look combined with conservative substance that'll keep it from ever appearing tired."

Jim chimed in, "This variety of regimental-rep ties adds flare. We'll include this black knit tie—it's very avant-garde!

"You know how to tie a regular knot?"

I nodded. Every Kamehameha boy knew that because we wore khaki ties daily, part of our CKC uniforms.

"Then I will teach you both a full and a half-Windsor knot as well. You'll have varied looks.

"Oh, and tuck a white handkerchief in the coat pocket like this—and like this—and like this. Flexibility adds variety," Jim said assuredly.

"This suit's flannel material will not wrinkle easily, it won't be expensive to maintain, and will always look good on you," Will promised.

They both seemed to be having a great time. Mother stayed in the background, looking rather awestruck as they converted me into "a gentleman."

"Try it on," Will urged, sort of nudging me toward the dressing room.

I was 6' 4" tall; the jacket's drape and broad shoulders made me appear formidable.

It became my "Power Suit" and was the secret of my being able to afford college.

The national college fraternity system came into existence at the college I chose. Spectacular stone houses looked like replicas of elegant mansions in beautiful Colonial Williamsburg, Virginia: old, traditional, elegant. Someone said wallpaper in the Alpha Delta Phi dining room—it was *the Alpha Chapter*—cost over $1 million.

I wore the "Power Suit" the McInerney Brothers selected for me when I visited fraternities during tours all freshmen were given. Its cut, styling, my accessory coordination all helped to create a dramatic impression, making me look as if I belonged to a sugar plantation owner's family—the kind of person they'd feel they could trust!

Some of fraternity house managers were eager to interview me. I would supervise taking care of the coal furnace that heated their fraternity house for much of the school year.

I promised, "We'll make you feel as cozy as if you're in Hawaii!" (No one else applying for that job would have such a memorable selling slogan.)

The McInerney Brothers had helped me to look like someone reliable—even when it's freezing.

"We" included "me, myself, and I"—but I didn't explain *that*.

I used the cellar door, and our work clothes–clad team (me, myself, and I) kept college boys comfortable even when the temperature dropped *way below zero*, which was often and lasted long. Those stone buildings didn't leak heat; two or three trips a day to shovel coal kept everyone cozy.

I always paid local workmen to haul away the ashes so me, myself, or I weren't seen in work clothes doing manual labor, such as pushing around filled garbage cans.

The twins established a foundation in Hawaii that assists young people to gain an education. I wanted you to know how their gentlemanly services helped make mine possible. Their adage endured throughout my business life: *Clothes make the man.*

27.

Sixtieth Reunion

The schools picked just borders,
Recruiting each island,
Pua they selected
Made a varied garland.

It was such a *small* school,
Serving poor *kanaka;*
"Cash it in," critics said:
"Your estate no mattah!'"

"Won't sell the Princess' land,"
Trustees told the Big Five,
"Though land-rich and cash poor,
Her dream needs to survive!"

Girls go to Boys' campus,
Wounded soldiers use theirs,
But invisible threads
Prevented co-ed "shares."

The class of 'forty-three
Seventeen girls, one boy—
Matched against other schools
We seemed a little toy.

Five-foot tall footballers,
120-pound linemen,
"Quack," who walked like a duck,
Ran for us around end.

Coach pled with recruiters:
"Judge boys by appetite;
We need to grow a team!
We'll feed eaters just right!"

Coach Mountain, looking down
On Bishop Museum
Saw new Kalihi Prep
He smiled, for this reason:

"Not room for more boarders?
Put those Preps on our bus
Let them come here daily,
Live at home—no big fuss."

"Pauahi's will be done;
Day scholars are in it,
Let them share in the fund
Enlargen and admit!

"Visit the junior highs,
With welcome mat on view:
'Greetings Honolulu,
Pauahi loves you, too!'"

"Days" brought new excitement,
Increasing our stature:
"A football championship!"
Being "bigger" was grander.

Now, the lei of flowers
With all islands' *pua,*
Glowing radiantly,
With lots of *ilima.*

Still, our numbers stayed small,
Our class' boys: sixty-five;
Same class at St. Louis:
One hundred eighty-five!

Abraham, Benjamin,
Joseph, Solomon, James—
Our class sounds Caucasian—
No Hawaiian first names!

Had our own "Joseph Smith"—
Don't shake your head askance;
All this was true back then,
Before "The Rennaisance."

Boys in school uniforms
Blue work clothes and khaki,
For "dress-up," girls wore white,
Symbolized purity.

Followed the middle road
No left or right byways,
Believed what teachers told,
Not "Doing Things My Way."

Puberty challenges
Say, faced in Milolii,
Somewhat different than ones
Girls have in Waikiki.

"With hilltop discipline,"
Dr. Frederick observes,
"'Days' aren't different than 'Nights,'
I'll fix their learning curves."

School shops made us ready
For local job demands,
In all skills be steady,
Earnest, have good work hands.

Senior Cottage girls learn
Marriage is not heaven;
Plan, cook, and baby care
That's "24/7."

Sew graduation gown:
"Finishing School Ladies"
With politeness renown,
Ready to raise babies.

Missionary concepts
Were the goals of that time:
Have a job, run a home
In a repressive clime.

Boys and girls learned to march,
Follow an honor code,
America challenged?
Come forward and be bold.

A salute from veterans,
Patriots all they be,
"The Great Generation"
Of God, Home, Country.

We've followed the school pledge
Throughout all our long lives:

Respecting our founder,
Meeting our potential,
Acting responsibly,
With dignity and pride!

Military

Hawaii is the headquarters for the U.S. military in the Pacific.
Those stationed here,
Those leaving here to serve elsewhere,
And family members here too,
Deserve Hawaii's understanding
And Aloha.

28.

Serving on Guano Piles

Beginning in 1935, the U.S. Army secretly assigned 170 Hawaii schoolboys to desolate islands to hinder England's expansion in the Pacific equatorial region.

The Army told the boys, "You will colonize and help establish claim to the Baker, Jarvis, and Howland Islands. They'll become famous air bases in a route to connect Australia and California."

A new documentary and traveling exhibit on this subject titled *Under a Jarvis Moon* was prepared under the aegis of the Bishop Museum. It expands on *Panalaau Memoirs,* written by E. H. Bryan Jr. in 1974, as well as an exhibit by the museum in 2002.

I knew some of the boys from boarding school and through family ties. One was the best friend of Captain David Lyman, late mariner and voyager cousin.

Their service in the Pacific was secret. Returning colonists were supposed to say, "We went south to study sea life for the Bishop Museum."

Some boys feared, groundlessly of course, being shot by the Army for talking about where they went and why.

I recall that each boy was paid $30 a month—good money then—to help their families (the same amount received by contemporaries in the Civilian Conservation Corps (CCC). That was bottom-line money; CCC boys were fed, clothed, and housed.) Boys on guano dumps didn't need much. Basic monthly pay in the U.S. Army was about $21.

Twelve students at a time were placed among the islands for six months. They were given 50-gallon drums of water and food staples. The ocean teemed with edible fish; it took about five minutes to step out on a reef and spear mullet and snapper for the day's meal.

Boys charted the weather, checked in with the Army by shortwave radio, read the school books they took with them, and waited for six months to end. Some reenlisted to help their families. Think jobs are hard now to find in Hawaii? It was worse then during the Great Depression.

Should curious Englishmen stop by, boys were to claim the islands as "their home" and radio the U.S. Army immediately.

They built a church and dedicated it to the memory of Amelia Earhart who, with Fred Noonan, had disappeared while flying to Howland Island, which is 1,700 miles southwest of Hawaii.

Jarvis, Howland, and Baker Islands were once valued for the guano deposits filled with phosphate that birds left there (the reason for the U.S. Guano Act of 1856). Other than having doo-doo from birds using islands as a nesting and roosting place, there was virtually nothing on the islands: treeless, sparse, only scattered grasses, vines, and low shrubs.

It was as unlike Michener's later fabled "Bali-Hai" as any place could be. (Michener was a great fiction writer, you know. Some of us call that kind of writing "faction"—blending facts and fiction.)

Two boys were killed during air raids and a submarine shelling at Howland Island on December 8, 1941. The Japanese shot down the American flag over the boys' "Amelia Earhart church."

A U.S. destroyer rescued the survivors in late January 1942.

Their adventure was over.

Britain's threat for choice Pacific flights and economic dominance in the Pacific was gone as well.

Survivors were tight-lipped. Back at school, all they said was "We've been away studying crabs."

29.

Secret at West Loch

We heard explosions from our hilltop, saw smoke rising, and watched ships escaping to sea. On May 21, 1944, boarding students at Kamehameha Schools believed enemy submarines had returned to Pearl Harbor.

The harbor was swollen with combat ships, cargo vessels, and even old World War I four-stackers. Something big was under way. And now this!

Because it was wartime, civilians were told nothing.

Many years later, I learned firsthand details from Henry Schramm when we worked together in Syracuse, New York. Schramm had been a seaman on a minesweeper that was back from January's Marshall Islands campaign.

It had joined a large task force of battlewagons, cruisers, landing ships, and troop carriers holding a major dress rehearsal off Maui for the invasion of Saipan. His minesweeper had returned to West Loch.

The fleet was there in Pearl because ships were loading war supplies prior to invading the Marianas. While other sailors were on shore leave, Schramm was on the bridge

147

reading at about 1430 hours. A sailor on watch rushed over.

"There's a base fire alert. Can you two-block the fire flag?"

He ran up the signal flag. In a few seconds, every ship at Pearl Harbor had raised signals on otherwise naked masts.

Schramm grabbed a pair of binoculars, scanned around the horizon, and watched as a gigantic explosion rocked the area.

A truck, then a jeep, rose above the blast, seemed to hang forever, then tumbled back into the inferno. Six LST landing ships loaded with ammunition exploded. Other normally land- or sea-based items—mostly large— made brief appearances as flying objects and then dropped from sight.

Because of all the explosives at Pearl, Schramm worried that the whole place would go up.

Someone said, "No, the big stuff is in the ammo depot near the harbor mouth."

Someone else added, "Mines and torpedoes are stored there," Schramm remembered.

With the rising crescendo of sirens and ships' horns, Schramm glimpsed a massive cloud of black smoke rising from West Loch. Huge orange flames flickered. Heavy smoke poured out of a large cargo ship. No tugs accompanied her; she appeared to be a runaway drifting toward that ammunition depot.

The cargo ship lost steerage and drove ever closer to the depot, probably a thousand yards away, then jolted to a stop. Apparently it had run aground in the one area from which it could do no damage to the base's stored explosives, nor would it block the channel. It continued to burn at a slower pace, losing the breeze from its forward motion.

Schramm returned to the binoculars and their view of a billowing black and orange foreground superimposed on a deep blue Hawaiian sky. He described it:

"The explosions continued, each new burst of flame accompanied by a distinctive boom, reaching us several seconds later. More and more of the northern sky was blotted out by the thick, oily clouds. Fireboats and seagoing tugs with high-pressure hose mounts proceeded up the channel with sirens going, cutting fierce wakes as they roared forward."

Ships headed out to sea, a remarkable feat by the few who were on board. Dozens of harbor craft began a grim parade from West Loch down the channel, skirting Ford Island, making for Fleet Landing. Shipmates returning from liberty witnessed the unloading of scores of bodies along the pier. Despite the minimal numbers of people aboard the ships, 163 were killed and 396 others were injured.

As darkness approached, Schramm looked to the northwest where fire still glowed. Higgins boats continued to trek toward the fire site and return with more depressing cargo.

In just six hours, hundreds of lives had been snuffed out or changed forever; millions of dollars in Navy ships and war materiel had been destroyed.

What caused the disaster? Initial thoughts went toward a Japanese suicide mission or sabotage.

Kamehameha seniors apprenticing at Pearl Harbor brought back a story circulating around the base that a Japanese welder had purposely set off anti-aircraft shells in an ammunition locker with sparks from his torch.

I satisfied my curiosity some 30 years later by obtaining a copy of the U.S. Navy's then-declassified investigation report. It stated that explosions actually originated from the cigarettes of servicemen working on the LSTs, who were roughly handling ammunition—including five-inch projectiles and phosphorous bombs—*while smoking!*

A prominent sign in the area stated, "No Smoking." No welding was being performed in the indicated areas of the initial explosion. There was no evidence of sabotage.

Hawaii was then under martial law, and local newspapers were censored. Consequently, all that appeared was a one-inch article informing local residents of "a minor fire at Pearl Harbor."

It was major enough to delay the Saipan invasion for a week.

That delay gave about 30,000 Americans and Japanese fighting men another week of life: That's the total of battle casualties.

30.

'I Shall Return'—But First . . .

Sixty-five years ago, soldiers from Hawaii helped General McArthur keep his promise to return to the Philippines.

"Queenie,"* General Charles Reed Bishop Lyman of Hawaii, joined his fellow West Pointer after leading preliminary operations in the Palaus, Leyte, and Luzon.

The Palau Islands—Angaur and Peleliu—had to be neutralized to protect McArthur's flank once his invasion began.

Japanese had changed their defense tactics and no longer used reckless Banzai attacks. They sought to draw Americans into a bloody war of attrition—relying on heavily fortified bunkers, caves, and underground positions.

Reduction of the Japanese pocket around Umurbrogol mountain on Peleliu was considered the most difficult fight that the U.S. military encountered in the Second World War. It lasted over two months and the National Museum of the Marine Corps describes it as "the bitterest battle of the war." Marine casualties were horrendous.

The Army's 81st Division arrived from Hawaii after their training in "Paradise."

Grunts on the sand called the new place "Paradise Lost."

The Japanese introduced a new trick on Angaur. As a pillbox-blowing squad approached, the Japanese soldiers inside would flee through rear entrances. In a tree behind the pillbox, one of them waited with a knee mortar braced against the trunk, zeroed in on the pillbox. When the tell-tale smoke of a demolition charge rose above the blown pillbox, the Japanese mortar coughed, and the men who had blown the pillbox and waited to see the results of their handiwork were slaughtered by the shell dropped in their midst.

Hawaii-trained soldiers arrived with tanks that bucked through the jungle—beautiful, rumbling, ponderous monsters with descriptive names: "Golgotha, Bloody Bucket, Singing Guns, Sea Breeze."

I was told this: "One spot buddies in the 81st will not forget was Bloody Gulch near Suicide Hill. A Japanese 75, mounted on rails so it could be fired and then retracted into a cave, whammed down projectiles. It had the gulch covered. When a tank was hit, its blazing hulk stopped the entire advance until demolition men, working without protection or cover, got rid of it."

GIs who'd poured into Beautiful Hawaii for stationing and training were in for an awful surprise from Nature while working their way through the Pacific.

Apart from the enemy were three major hazards in the Palaus: insects, terrain, and climate. Insects were like something out of a psychotic nightmare. Mosquitoes were bad, but you got accustomed to them and could tolerate them. It was the endless variety of other bug life that made field-living hell. They worried you in your spare time, they slept with you at night, and they ate with you and on you.

In a loathsome category all their own were the shiny, black worms that were always falling from the sides of foxholes, walls, and shelter halves, too clumsy and heavy to support their own repulsive bodies.

Varying in length from four to eight inches, about as big around as your little fingers, trotting along on their multitudinous feet looking like animated weenies dipped in axle grease, they were right out of a DT's morning after. When one landed on you, the shudder started in your GI brogans and ended up rattling your eyeballs.

For fighting purposes, the terrain was about the worst that could have been conceived in Beelzebub's fiendish mind. The jungle smothered body and spirit, and the Japanese were able to take advantage of pinnacles which formed crazed patterns and provided deep rents in the tortured landscape. The enemy had caves with entrances that couldn't be forced by troops farther away than grenade-throwing range.

But above all, it was the almost unbearable heat that made the Palaus so tough.

The sun beat down in a brassy, oppressive glare. Any slight exertion sent rivulets of perspiration down beneath already sweat-soured shirts.

A man could lie down without doing a thing and feel his forehead beading up as the water popped out. Although salt tablet instructions call for not more than

15 a day, on Angaur and Peleliu they frequently took as many as 30.

They'd carry two canteens of water ashore, but water was a problem. There wasn't any potable water on Angaur. It had to be ferried in from ships that brought it from Hawaii.

Hawaii had cooling trade winds, flowers, greenery, abundant pure water, and no slithery wormy critters. It was "Paradise" in the Pacific.

After retiring from the Army, Uncle Charlie Lyman raised racehorses in West Chester, Pennyslvania, on his "Maui Hills Farms."

Uncle Charlie described what happened after General McArthur waded ashore at Leyte in the Philippines on October 1944 and told the press, "I have returned."

"Down from their mountain camps to meet us came some frightening looking, but welcome allies." He said Clayton M. Rollins of Southington, Connecticut, and Clement J. Novinski of Wilkes-Barre, Pennsylvania, led American-Filipino guerrilla forces.

"Escaping from the Bataan 'Death March' in the dark days of 1941, they helped lead units of fierce Igorot fighters, equipped with a variety of Japanese, American, and Filipino homemade rifles, in hundreds of forays against Japanese garrisons and supply points."

Uncle Charlie explained, "U.S. Army men escaping to the hills wore Filipino clothes, went barefoot when their shoes wore out, and got so brown that only the blond-haired guys could be taken for Americans."

They probably resembled California surfers who hang out on Oahu's North Shore.

*Brothers Three: Brig. General Charles Reed Bishop Lyman, Big Island born and raised, earned Silver and Bronze Stars for leading operations in New Guinea, Leyte, and Luzon. Charles (#5188), with older brothers Albert (#4764) and Clarence (#4382), were the first part-Hawaiians to attend West Point! They may have been its first non-Caucasians. Uncle Charles was proud to be in the infantry; Clarence, a cavalry captain, died during World War I. Brig. General Albert Kualii, Army engineer, died during World War II.

Queen Liliuokalani and Queen Emma asked "the Lyman Boys" to send all their report cards to them. Fellow cadets nicknamed Charles "Queenie" because the queen sent him so many Hawaiian gold coins, rewards for high grades.

31.

Welcome Home, USS Hawaii

As our state's namesake sub slipped in for the first time, Kamehameha alumni glee clubbers sang patriotic and heroic songs in Hawaiian; it was part of our statewide display of pride.

"Hole Waimea," one of the songs, is based on Kamehameha the Great's fierce warriors' chant. Its richly blended harmonic chorus illustrates a successful outcome when those of valor work together.

Appropriate introduction for the ceremony, wouldn't you say, as USS *Hawaii* smoothly slipped in to its new home port?

Stick up for America, wrote a college friend in Groton, Connecticut, where the sub was built. He responded to my proud news, passing along some patriotic reminders I've rephrased.

At a time when our president and other politicians tend to apologize for prior actions, these serve as refreshers on how others handled negative comments about our country.

President John F. Kennedy's secretary of state, Dean Rusk, was in France in the early sixties when de Gaulle decided to pull out of NATO. De Gaulle said he wanted all U.S. military out of France as soon as possible!

Rusk responded, "Does that include those who are buried here?"

That tall, domineering Frenchman looked down without responding.

When Colin Powell was in England, at a fairly large conference, the Archbishop of Canterbury asked "If our plans for Iraq were just an example of empire-building by George Bush."

Powell replied: "Over the years, the United States has sent many fine young men and women into great peril to fight for freedom beyond our borders. The only amount of land we have ever asked for in return is enough to bury those that did not return."

A number of international company technical experts were at a conference in France. After a break, a French engineer returned to the room and said:

"Have you heard the latest dumb stunt Bush has done? He has sent an aircraft carrier to Indonesia to help the tsunami victims. What does he intended to do, bomb them?" (Smirk, smirk.)

A Boeing engineer stood up; he replied quietly:

"Our carriers have three hospitals on board that can treat several hundred people; they are nuclear powered and can supply emergency electrical power to shore facilities; they have three cafeterias with the capacity to feed 3,000 people three meals a day, they can produce several thousand gallons of fresh water from sea water each day, and they carry half a dozen helicopters for use in transporting victims and injured to and from their flight deck.

"We have eleven such ships. How many does France have?"

Silence.

A U.S. Navy admiral was at a naval conference that included admirals from the English, Canadian, Australian, and French Navies. At a cocktail reception, he found himself standing with a large group of officers from those countries.

Everyone was chatting away in English as they sipped their drinks, when a French admiral suddenly complained:

"Whereas Europeans learn many languages, Americans learn only English."

He then asked, "Why is it that we always have to speak English in these conferences rather than speaking French?"

Without hesitating, the American admiral replied, "Maybe it's because the Brit's, Canadians, Aussie's, and Americans arranged it so you wouldn't have to speak German."

Robert Whiting, elderly gentleman of 83, arrived in Paris by plane. At French Customs, he took a few minutes to locate his passport in his carry-on.

"You have been to France before, monsieur?" sarcastically asked the customs officer.

Mr. Whiting admitted he had been to France previously.

"Then you should know enough to have your passport ready."

The American said, "The last time I was here, I didn't have to show it."

"Impossible! Americans always have to show a passport on arrival in France."

The American senior gave the Frenchman a long, hard look, then quietly explained:

"Well, when I came ashore at Omaha Beach on D-Day in 1944 to help liberate this country, I couldn't find a single Frenchman to show a passport to."

Americans have others who criticize us; these old chestnuts about allies we twice helped pull out of the fire happened to be on the top of my list.

Welcome to your new home, USS *Hawaii* crew members!

Happy shore leave! We witnessed joy on your family members' faces as your nuclear submarine slipped in.

We're glad this is now your home base. Please know that Hawaii is proud of you.

32.

Awake in the Deep

Focus, deep patience from gifted mindset.
Is what we observed while under the deck,
Seeing the sailors in their submarine,
Now, Pearl Harbor's newest nuclear machine.

The U.S. Pacific Fleet admiral
In the shipyard commissioned this new sub,
"Arrival Day," at its home terminal
We sang as it slid in smoothly and snug.

Admiral Roughead said, "Come on aboard—
Show them around, Captain, it's their reward."
Seeing waiting wives made us hesitate,
"Could we do that, Sir, on another date?"

Asking that, gave us a sub full of fans.
Two weeks later we were picked up by vans,
Commander Herrington served as our guide
Explaining everything we'd see inside.

J. Arthur Rath III

Down a metal ladder, inching our way,
Where you can't tell if'n it's night or day—
Actually it seemed like twilight down there.
Good fresh smell from the circulating air.

Without crouching, sort of standing up tall,
No claustrophobe or strange feeling at all.
Smiling commander welcomed us "On Board,"
Began orienting us, straight forward:

"$2.5 billion for this 'brand-new world,'
370-feet long, top banner unfurled,
Not to make war, but to help ensure peace.
At sea its vigilance will never cease.

"Part of the Navy's first line of defense,
Primary task being 'intelligence.'
Underwater for months tracking a foe,
Stealthily offshore, guarding against woe.

Won't surface, never seen, we're always there.
Limitless power makes water and air."
Life is compressed within this submarine,
It's an integrated fighting machine:

Missiles, torpedoes strike with precision,
Well supplied with lots of ammunition.
Anti-submarine, mine warfare resort,
Special forces delivery and support.

Confident manner of the alert crew,

Showed how to duty every one is true.
The bright eyes, ready smile on all we meet,
Made me ask: "Do you recruit the elite?"

The proud commander smiled real merrily:
"They are all above average as you see,
Engineering training helps each excel
Because our atmosphere is technical,
Optimism and gentlemanly grace
Works best when you live with limited space,
And have little time to eat or to sleep."

Around the clock and seven days a week,
Six hours of work, four hours of sleep,
Every day's the same—and the sleeping loft
Where what's called the "Hot Bunks" never cools off:
Four hours and then down, another's up,
Crowded six bunks could fit in a closet.
Line up for meals, have five minutes to eat,
Don't delay: Someone's waiting for your seat!

Enchiladas, pizza, hamburgers, too,
Along with other stuff that's good for you.
Officers' 45-minute dining—
Encourages conversational thriving.

Soup, salad, entrée, and dessert delight
(Can't start until the commander's first bite).
Don't chew faster than the commander does—
Otherwise you'll see frowns, hear others' buzz.

Shower regimen for the outer man,

Turn on tap, wet down, turn tap off, soap up,
Rub in shampoo turn tap back on, and rinse
Out within five minutes, others want in.
(Over too fast, no time to rhyme.)

That summarizes the glimpses I gleaned
While touring Hawaii's new submarine.
The sub's commander, along with its crew,
Wives and children are new residents too.

Commander Edward Herrington's own prose,
Expresses what the crew feels and knows,
Here they're excerpted by an e-mail muse
From his en route to Honolulu views:

*"We hope the festive ceremony for our arrival sets the
tone for the relationship we desire to maintain with the local
community over the next thirty years.* [Author: This is the
anticipated service life of the USS *Hawaii.*]

*"Most of our families are now arriving in Hawaii.
Moving can be quite stressful, especially ones with small
children. . . . Families have been sharing stories about how
welcome they have felt and how wonderful the weather and
scenery has been. . . . Having our families waiting on the
pier for us when we arrive will make the homecoming that
much more special.*

*"The crew has been watching a nightly movie together.
This week two of the movies had scenes filmed in Hawaii.
Everyone was really excited about the scenes and how
breathtaking everything is. . . . Sailors serving previously*

in Hawaii rave about how wonderful all of the golf courses are.

"I have the weather in Hawaii saved on my iphone and check it frequently to remind myself of how nice it is going to be once we arrive at our new home."

These are the first of new Navy neighbors
Who'll add their part to Hawaii flavors.
Our world of defense has changed mightily,
Some of the most vital are under sea.
John Dyke's melody for "The Navy Hymn"—
For our new neighbors, these words fit right in:
"Lord God, our power evermore,
Whose arm doth reach the ocean floor,
Dive with our men beneath the sea;
Traverse its depths protectively,
Oh hear us when we pray and keep
Them safe from peril in the deep."

Adding for their families now with us,
Quietly, bravely, without any fuss:
Bless them at home who wait and pray
For their return, by night or day.

33.

Manny and the Many Hooneys

Service families and other island newcomers live among kamaaina in our Aiea housing complex. Friendships sometimes begin at poolside.

I met Manfred Gessler while his mother sunned herself.

He trotted over saying:

"I'm Manny; you're always reading a book. What's that one about?"

I looked inquiringly at his mother with whom I'd previously spoken. They moved here shortly after her husband's New Jersey National Guard unit transferred to Schofield; Lt. Gessler was assigned to Iraq.

Mrs. Gessler nodded, so I paid attention to Manny. Slight, with dark curly hair, huge sparkling eyes, and a quick, eager smile, he appeared to be about nine years old.

"I'm rereading it, Manny. It's a reissue of *Ben-Hur* by Civil War general Lew Wallace. A modern-day artist named Warren Chang did the drawings. See this one of the Roman cheating in the chariot race?"

"Please explain."

I began, having finally learned to stop explaining things when others' eyes glaze.

"Ben-Hur was a Jew who lost all he had. Brave and loyal, he impressed the sheik of Syria, who said: 'I think better of thee, son of Israel, thou shalt have the horses in the morning.'"

Manny's mother smiled, so I continued.

"Ben-Hur harnessed the sheik's white Arabian horses to his chariot. In a big race in the Coliseum he defeated the arrogant Roman and became a famous hero. Ben-Hur made friends with the three Wise Men who traveled to see Baby Jesus just after he was born. (I thought it was okay to say this to him because of the holiday season.)

"Those kings were from Turkey, Saba, and also Iran— which is near where your Dad is stationed."

Still having his attention, I added local flavor.

"December 7 was on a Sunday again this year. When I was your age I lived close to Pearl Harbor at the time a person from the small island of Saba became an American hero—Balthazar was the Wise Man who came from there.

"As enemy torpedo planes attacked, this hero released the Battleship Nevada from the mooring so it wouldn't block the harbor entrance. He jumped into the water, swam after it, climbed aboard, and continued the fight using its triple gun turrets.

He was awarded the Naval Cross."

Manny's mother brought over a bag of cookies. After some crunching, he put my harbor story into his own perspective:

"Mr. Klotz said oysters people ate sometimes contained pearls."

"Pearl gathering in Pearl Harbor stopped a very long time ago, Manny. Who is Mr. Klotz?"

"Samuel Klotz is my new Hawaii grandpa. He's an outpatient at Tripler Hospital where Mama works and he lives near school. I wait at his house for Mama to drive me home.

"I'm in the third grade at Saint Elizabeth School. We wear blue uniforms because we're 'true blue.'"

Responding to my surprised look, he explained:

"The principal told Mama it's okay for a Jew to enroll as long as we accept the school's philosophy. It's much better than my old school in Passaic. The many Hooneys are my best friends and we play on weekends.

"Laura, Jessica, and Colin Hooney are ahead of me. Thomas is in my third-grade class, Michael is in the first grade. Lil' Patrick's not quite ready for school. They're from Iowa and their dad's in Iraq with mine.

"Mr. Klotz sits in a wheelchair and has a scary dragon on his one leg. He says,

'That leg was draggin' after an explosive from a howitzer landed near my foxhole during the Korean War, but its tattoo was my charm.'

"Losing most of his hearing, he learned how to sign. I speak right up. He hears me.

"Am I old enough to read Ben-Hur?"

"You certainly are!"

I met Manny and his mother on the elevator a few days later. I live on the first floor, but he'd already pushed his floor's button.

I'd spotted him studying the Aiea Public Library's holiday display yesterday; it featured books about Christmas, Hanukkah, Japanese New Year, and Kwanzaa—the newer African-American holiday. The ride up gave me the chance to hear his thoughts.

"Kwanzaa makes me think of Hanukkah at grandma's," he said. "Our family also lights a candle each night of the week and talks about doing good things.

"Here's the 16th floor, goodbye."

I didn't see Manny until a few days before New Year's, at poolside. Motioning to the eating area, Mrs. Gessler handed me a paper plate with latke—garnished potato pancakes—and ice-cold green tea. She returned to the chaise lounge. Manny and I talked. It was before noon, and we had the covered patio all to ourselves.

Now *he* was the storyteller:

"First, you should understand that Mr. Klotz knows everything about Aiea," he began.

Manny doesn't require verbal responses.

"His dad was a Filipino cook on a U.S. Navy warship. 'Frangipani,' the family name, was too long for the sailors. They called him 'Klutz' because of his broken English.

"An officer said he cooked too good to be called that and renamed him 'Klotz.'

"Even then, Mr. Sumida hired people from the Philippines for his watercress farm.

"After the war the Frangipanis moved here, worked with watercress, and became Klotzes."

I added, "Aiea was a breadbasket because of its rich soil and artesian wells. Taro, rice, and other crops grew here.

"American settlers bored wells into water-bearing layers of rock. The hills' angle produced a constant supply of water with little or no pumping. This made sugarcane fields possible.

"Plantations later sold their land. Aiea became what it is now. The nearby Sumida Watercress Farm reminds us that good food can be grown here."

Manny was more interested in his recent events than in my detailed history.

"I want to tell you about Samuel Klotz and Christmas.

"But first you should know I'm excited about Hawaii's next holidays."

"You mean New Year's Eve and the fireworks?"

"Yes, but Japanese New Year is also new for me. I think some classmates are sending cards.

"Grandma Rubenstein is coming, and we're taking her to a Japanese New Year's dinner. Then it'll be Chinese New Year and we'll see a real dragon in the Chinatown parade.

"Grandma used to say 'We eat Chinese.'" He giggled. "She meant 'weekly take-out,' because in her kosher house there is no cooking on the Shabbat. We'll go to a Ding Sung Restaurant.

"Hawaii has so many holiday flavors!"

"Manny, are you going to tell me about Christmas with Samuel Klotz?"

"Oh, yes, yes, yes! That's when I witnessed the Christmas Vision."

I may have looked puzzled, but he continued.

"Mama drove me over to Mr. Klotz' on Christmas afternoon. I brought a bottle of kosher wine made from grapes grown in high elevations of the Upper Galilee.

"Mr. Klotz told me about old-time Hawaiian life here.

"There were ancient villages where shopping malls are now. Ewa Beach and Pearl Harbor were famous for good fishing.

"He said Aiea was enchanted."

"Yes, Manny, and remnants remain: A wild pig occasionally appears in a neighborhood. After a moonlight night, little fairy rings from their dancing can be seen at dawn on golfing greens."

The look on his face was a clue Manny had lots more to tell me.

"Please continue," I said.

"Mr. Klotz fell asleep. Bushes behind his porch began shaking. I heard noises sounding like mynah birds.

"A small person popped out, laid down some items, and scooted away. Another came out and did the same thing. Then another.

"I nudged Mr. Klotz. As he opened his eyes, the little men reappeared.

One carried a small American flag. Another held a piece of cardboard on which was pasted a newspaper photograph of young Barack Obama sitting on the Punahou lawn with classmates.

"Out stepped the third one. After making sure he had our attention, he moved his arms and made finger signs.

"Mr. Klotz nodded in agreement, and the three little men went back into the bushes.

"He explained to me: 'The menehune used universal sign language realizing you and I wouldn't understand Hawaiian. They delivered this holiday greeting:

""Peace on earth. Good will to all mankind."'

"'It's what Angels sang on the first Christmas. They want you to know the world will change. And your father will be home soon from lands near where the Wise Men traveled to see the newborn Jesus.'"

"As he finished, I heard joyful sounds coming up the road. Not from menehune—it was the many Hooneys.

"They shrieked with excitement when seeing presents from the little people:

"'Oh! . . . Ling Hing Mui! . . . Moochi! . . . Manapua! . . . Krispy Kreme!'

"In a loud, slow voice, Mr. Klotz summed up everything:

"'Mele Kalikimaka is the thing to say On a bright Hawaiian Christmas Day.'"

"I have to go, Manny. You are inspiring. Mazel tov, little pal."

Grinning, he responded:

"I go to Saint Elizabeth, I'm true blue, becoming 'local' too, and now can greet you in both ways:

"Hauoli Makahiki Hou! Happy New Year!"

34.

Punchbowl Cemetery Musings

Sixty-four years ago, as the Battle of Okinawa wound down, the Military High Command anticipated one million U.S. invasion casualties in months ahead.

The *legendary* factor wasn't even considered:

For six and a half centuries, protected by Kamikaze, the divine wind, Japan had never been successfully invaded.

Had peace not been signed in August 1945, the U.S. invasion fleet—thousands of ships, planes, landing craft, and a half million men—would have been in that exact place poised to attack at the exact time in October when Typhoon Louise enveloped Okinawa and surrounding seas.

This furious and lethal storm, with winds rising to 100 mph and waves 60 feet high, devastated everything in its path.

If "Operation Downfall"—the invasion's code name—was in position as planned, Hawaii's Punchbowl would be overflowing.

"The War to End All Wars"
It's what your fathers fought,
Yours evolved from that one—
And imperious pride.
Old-timers still point out:
"Planes came over mountains
Through that pass there, slashing
Toward ships in Pearl Harbor."

Fast convoys left San Fran.
With you and other troops:
Jones, Goldstein, Skorski, Smith—
Fine American names
On the stones I see here.

You came in olive drab
To build World War II's road:
Hawaii to Tokyo,
Three-thou, four-hundred miles,
With stops along the way.

Once an outer bastion,
Oahu's a springboard—
Supply base, nerve center,
The Mid-Pac command post.
Three-hundred thousand "yous"
In Jungle Training School,
Oahu, Maui's surf,
Land with full pack and gun.

Learn "Jungle Survival"
At Bishop Museum
Should you be marooned
. . . When your plane has no gas,
. . . If the boat you're on sinks,
. . . You're the last left alive.

"The Pacific Crossroads":
It's where you leave to fight,
To return if wounded,
Check in here for furlough,
A final resting place.

War began and will end
Around Honolulu,
Shipping from its harbor
Ten million tons cargo
For Pacific warriors.

Each amphibious man
Has nine ton of supplies
To sustain his first days—
Then, a long ton a month.

6/21 Okinawa's done,
An 82-day war,
50k GIs down—
100k enemy,
One-quarter civilians.

Battle stories are grim,
They are hidden within,
We view just the outside.
Optimistic GIs
Jones, Goldstein, Skorski, Smith—
Fine American names
On the stones I see here.

Your trip to "Paradise:"
War in the Pacific,
Before Enola Gay*

* On August 6, 1945, "Enola Gay," a B-29 Superfortress
bomber, dropped "Little Boy," the first atomic bomb,
on Hiroshima. Three days later, "Bockscar," another
B-29, dropped "Fat Man," a second nuclear weapon on
Nagasaki. An immediate flurry of negotiations began.
Twenty-four days later, Japan formally surrendered and
World War II was over.

Insights

When I was a boy, an elderly malo-clad Hawaiian man known as "David of Punaluu" lived in a grass shack and off the land, as had his ancestors.

Time stood still for him.

His shack was near the main highway that went around the island. Lots of people stopped in to see him and be charmed.

Welcoming visitors, he spoke these verses vagabond Don Blanding had attributed to him (or maybe it was vice versa):

With a laugh on my lips at dawning,
With a song and a heart to sing,
With the sun and the moon for neighbors,
I'm richer than any king.

It is *not quite* that way today for modern Hawaii's homeless.

Proceeds from sales of *Slices of Life in Hawaii* volume 1 go to organizations that help feed them. It's book-buyer and publisher *kokua.**

Kokua: Hawaiian noun and verb for help, aid, assistance.

179

35.

Prodigal Son

Classmate Moses, pure Hawaiian, grew up on Kauai; his large, old-fashioned-style Hawaiian family lived near the river, close to the beach. Social life revolved around the nearby church.

He sowed wild oats for many years after high school graduation. "My, could he and Billy drink," is how a classmate described these two "Sunshine Boys."

Billy's now gone; he joined the Mormon church, started his own business in California, and became a bishop.

Moses found his way to Seattle, Washington, and deteriorated through self-indulgence. Many, many years later this prodigal returned to take care of the old family home. He'd experienced a profound change.

A couple of years ago I saw him with his elder brother at a memorial service. His one-time effervescence had been replaced with a shy, sweet smile and a quiet, humble voice. I felt a glow being in his presence. Moses had that quality.

A close friend who grew up on Kauai attended Moses' old-time Hawaiian-style funeral service and told me about it: hymn singing, *pule* (prayers), a reading from the Bible, and impromptu reflections from the congregation.

Moses exemplified St. Luke, Chapter 15: 11–32, the story of "The Prodigal Son"—the brother who was lost and became found.

That text was not used for the service—it would have been a little "much." And, anyway, the Biblical story doesn't end decisively.

Our Moses' later years exemplify good deeds that may have also resulted after the original Prodigal returned.

No one knew about lives remorseful Moses became responsible for until the service was about over. A young, neatly dressed white man, sitting in the back of the church with his wife and a child, walked hesitantly to the front platform to quietly say:

"I want you to know what Moses did for us.

"My wife and I were homeless and living on the beach in front of his place. Moses would come to see us. He convinced us it would be safer for us to sleep in his yard. He let us use his bathroom, outdoor shower, and washing machine. He often fed us. Although he had little, he shared. We picked fruit from his trees."

The church was so quiet by now that the young man's gentle voice filled it.

"My wife went into sudden labor and he delivered our baby. I just boiled the water. That's her and my daughter over there."

He pointed to his radiant wife sitting next to a three-year-old with golden ringlets on which the sun glistened like a halo.

He finished: "I followed Moses' advice—life became better for us."

My story of Moses concludes the same way as Luke 15 does:

Be glad. For this thy brother was lost and is found.

36.

Inscrutable

Hawaiian males project an outward guise,

Hiding deep emotions we feel inside.

So we use others' words to express love,

Singing, remaining stoical above.

. . . Dreams of the old days:
Silver of moons moving over nights.
The flesh-warm sand
In the dark embrace of moon and stars,
Gleaming in deep nocturnal blue.
Long-limbed palms of Waialae
Swaying in sea-curved arches.
Hovering hau of Kahala.
Cool, green-tinged kukui at Punahou.

. . . Leaf-moulding ravines
Heavy wild ginger upon Tantalus.
Koa with fern-damp shoulders
Cresting over Nuuanu.
Corners of hills and high hidden valleys
Cupping in Koolau hollows.
Seeing and feeling: We know of it all,
Less vulnerable with music's recall:
Pick and strum with powerful expression,
Enhance with falsetto for diversion.

Hiding in melody and words of grace;
While singing we keep our emotions safe.

Oahu's sisters, too, are part of him,
Quietly admired, they're his paean:

. . . Fire-blood summits glow on the young island of Hawaii,
Haleakala's gutted crest on Maui is
Magenta-dewed in its ash-cold bowl;
Molokai stretches her yawning cliffs
to the sky;
Lanai and Kahoolawe lie in the calm-cool
pools of sun;
Over Waialeale's hulk, a conflagration of clouds
rise out of the tundra of Kauai's plateaus;
Whisper-flung shadows of mountain and
cloud browse over Niihau on the
undulate bosom of the ocean.
Singing is our way to conjure past life,
Contained, while escaping all current strife.

. . . The rain-corroded dome of Koko Head
warming to the first soft brush of the sun.
The slate-toned crenellations of the Koolaus
kindling to purple, amethyst, and plum;
Morning stippling the pillars of Diamond Head
with patches of splendor;
Over the Waikiki roofs, facets of light
leaping onto Kawaiahao's grandeur.
Dawn sighs, wistful in its flight,
wandering on, wondering on,
following night.

It's over. We sigh, peaceful and sublime.
We'll sing to you again some other time.

37.

Optimistic Older Men

J ust received an invitation to join the alumni choir back East at this year's college reunions. The male group will sing selections from their youth, including *The Winds Are All Hushed . . . like a queen on her throne.*

It's the same weekend our high school has its reunion. Instead of singing about an ephemeral queen, we male alumni glee club members will wink, thinking we're appealing to earth-bound females. Delusional, but then so are most vain males.

We'll introduce a new arrangement of "Mi Nei."

"Mi" means the same as the English word "me". *"Nei"* turns it into the optimistic phrase "How About Me?"

While eastern college old-timers reminisce about times past, we're flirting here and now.

A reflection on outlooks may differ from where it's cold to where it's tropical.

At the alumni luau, we'll introduce an arrangement by Aaron Mahi. Hawaiian makes words to "Mi Nei" sound poetic and sweet.

But here is the translation of what the old geezers are *actually* saying:

You are searching all about
Wanting to fulfill the desire within,
Toward the mountains toward the sea, here and there
You search to fill the desire.
How would it be if it were right here?

You should gaze at this beauty.
These cheeks of mine
Are for you very fragrant.
Back straight like the cliffs from round like the moon,
Into these arms you come, we will be warm.
These eyes seize the heart.

When we kiss, you're at ease, I'm at ease.
"These arms, these shoulders of mine
Glance this way, below is the beauty
Brought forth and handled gently.

You will surely fancy what you see.
Tell the refrain, my glue has caught you
Aha! You're taken, taken by me!

Hope remains eternal in Hawaii males' breast.
It's good to be a sunshine boy again.

38.

Why Jewish Tourists Love Hawaii

I spotted a financial bonanza for hometown Honolulu during my first visit to Miami, Florida, in the early 1960s:

Acres of bodies sprawled on beaches and outside of hotels, the aroma of suntan oil rose from them.*

My Jewish boss and most of our clients returned from Florida with a winter tan. It identified them as financially more successful than pale-faced hoi polloi being slammed by winter while they basked in the sun.

Tan was thought to be sexy as well as prestigious. Ads in subway cars read "QT tans like magic in 3 to 5 hours with or without sun." It gave me an orange tinge.

Back at Waikiki, there's never a discouraging word and the skies are not cloudy all day. Miami and the eastern shore are flat, literally and figuratively, compared to multifaceted Hawaii.

It happened so quickly: Huge, fast airplanes disgorged tourists, travel costs dropped, it became convenient to fly from the East Coast. The Hawaii Visitors Bureau crowed about their promotions' "impacts on bottom lines" while the Hawaiian Islands metamorphosed into a mass-market tourism-based economy.

A faithful niche within that market has more "aloha" for Hawaii than many might realize. I thought about this after saying "Happy Hanukkah" to a cheerful family at the next table.

It was Friday evening at Kincaid's Fish, Chop, and Steak House in Waikiki. The TGIF "Thank God It's Friday" crowd worshipped at the bar.

I'd made reservations for a quick gimlet and broiled ahi before heading up to the University of Hawaii for Bamboo Ridge's party. It featured a reading by author Michelle Cruz Skinner, a born-and-raised Filipina.

At the long table next to us, 20 exuberant ladies enjoyed their Christmas Party. Two tables ahead sat a Jewish family who blessed and shared wine. It was the day before Hanukkah and I said "Happy Holiday" when leaving. They smiled back.

That simple exchange inspired me to write this message:

"Hawaii is an outstanding welcoming place and Aloha is the formula for a rewarding vacation. This perspective gives Jewish families more reason than ever to visit us. Tell the orthodox, for whom life is a little more demanding, '*kokua*'(cooperation) is here."

Although a Christian of Hawaiian ancestry, my insight was sharpened through years among Jews in New

York City and the Catskill Borscht Belt during its prime, as well as in Canada and most major American cities.

History

Jews are one of Hawaii's smallest minorities—about half of one percent of the population—but they settled here early. Paul Neumann was an adviser, friend, and legal counsel to King Kalakaua and advised the king's sister Queen Liliuokalani.

Jews, early merchants and importers, sold rice, sugar, coffee, and other island products. A number of outstanding Jewish-owned companies existed prior to annexation in 1898. It was when retail storekeeping became monopolized by Japanese and Chinese that most Jewish inhabitants left.

Requirements

With help from the Internet and hotel concierge, visitors find both services and dietary needs here.

Orthodox services are held in Waikiki at the Ala Moana Hotel. Oahu has Conservative and Reform services. Maui has Orthodox and Reformed services, and an Orthodox rabbi is on the Big Island.

No hotels in Hawaii keep kosher kitchens, but Oahu Kosher's "Yudi" will deliver food with a smile. Chef Yudi Weinbaum offers fully prepared meals and kosher catering on Oahu, Maui, Kauai, and the Big Island of Hawaii.

Added Value

Put a good mind to work and what do you get? A grand vacation!

Cousin Nelson Wong in Syracuse said he was going to cook for me and some friends. "Is lobster okay?" You bet!

After claws were cracked, we relaxed with wine. Nelson said his friend Seymour and wife were visiting Hawaii and wanted to borrow some books for background.

"How many?" I asked.

"We're interested in most everything," Seymour replied.

I brought a box full and said: "Return them when you return."

Three months later they showed me their trip report: It included museums, art galleries, historic places—and not just the usual ones—visits on four islands and to the volcano. They went to see Hawaii Preparatory Academy—"To gain an idea of Nelson's boyhood," Seymour explained.

He showed me notes he had written before and after the trip.

"This looks like a graduate-level course to Hawaii," I said.

"Seymour, I forgot your last name. . . ."

"Kaplan."

"SAT Kaplan?" I asked in astonishment. He'd prepared a cram course on Hawaii?

"No, Seymour Kaplan," he answered. "As a doctor I'm trained to be methodical."

That's something to realize: Jews represent a cadre of tourists eager for art, history, and learning who'll come methodically prepared with more information than some locals know.

Seymour perceived: *Hawaii is a repository of everything the mind and senses will enjoy.*

(Maybe I should trademark that phrase.)

Here for Fun

For many Jews, the mind works during the day, the senses play at night. Some of the best nightclub acts in the world performed in the Catskills when the Borscht Circuit attracted show business's best names. You know who nurtures the entertainment industry. Hawaii has loads of talent to share.

Opportunity may be sitting right over there with the big smile.

Jews will encourage chefs to exploit their skills, telling the server: *We want the best you can offer!*

I talked with Don Ho before his first big engagement in New York City, before he "hit it" nationally.

"Any tips about this audience, pal?" he asked.

"They'll really enjoy you," I answered. "I have only one suggestion. When you raise your glass and want everyone to join you in a drink, say the words *Suck 'Em Up* very distinctly. Otherwise they might think you are making a Yiddish slur." And then I said it.

"Ooo. . . . Those expressions do sound alike," he said. "Arthur, I'll make sure they hear me say three words—no confusion with one sounding insulting."

Jewish grandmothers were among the first in line to dance for Hawaii's tourism exemplar. Ho and Hawaii meant fun!

Our state is appreciated for being cosmopolitan and open-minded in other ways, too:

Local politics aren't subject to ethnic whims.
Just consider where our governor daily swims:
The Young Men's Christian Association pool,
Straight thinking and chutzpah distinguishes her rule.
'Cause here a free mind has many options to choose—
That is Hawaii's identity to Jews.

*Ron Rice, Daytona, Florida-based school teacher, visited Hawaii, discovered coconut, *kukui,* avocado, and other ingredients, returned home, mixed up a batch of suntan oil in a garbage can, and branded it Hawaiian Tropic ®. Rice drove to beaches and pool decks selling bottles of his "natural deep-tanning product." With a flair for promotion and running beauty pageants, he built a business now grossing over $200 million.

Culture and Community

La'akea Suganuma shares "mysterious things" in this section's first article. He's an *olohe lua aiwaiwa* (Hawaiian fighting arts instructor) and Hawaiian weapons expert.

I feel inextricably interwoven to his story:

La'akea's late mother, Pele, was my classmate and friend.

His grandmother Mary Kawena Pukui, was my mother's friend.

Mrs. Pukui was helpful and kind when I was an earnest young student and helped me get a job at the Bishop Museum that changed my life.

He is mystically connected to antecedents. I'm known as a bit fey.

What La'akea describes is told in the old-fashioned Hawaiian way, encompassing now and then along with those who never *really* go away.

Author's note: I didn't indicate an *okina* or glottal stop in other *Slices of Life* stories because I believe many readers outside of Hawaii may not be familiar with seeing words punctuated that way. As this book may be an introduction to Hawaii for some, I follow the older stylistic road that is well traveled—no *okina* between vowels. An example of the newer written use is to write "Hawai'i" instead of the more familiar "Hawaii."

This story by La'akea is an exception that includes *okina*. He is related to two fine Hawaiian language scholars, Mary Kawena Pukui and Pat Bacon (Namaka), both recognized for distinguished careers with the Bishop Museum. I show the *okina* (') as he learned it and use it to demonstrate how Hawaiian is now being published. That new approach is to aid pronunciation.

Kuhi dances with her grandmother's ipu.

39.

Hula with Ancestors

This is about a young woman's journey to become Miss Aloha Hula 2008. I say, with certainty, it began well before she was born.

My mother, Pele Puku'i Suganuma, was an expert hula dancer and chanter; her mother, Mary Kawena Puku'i, is considered the past century's foremost authority on Hawaiian culture.

Kawena's mother, Keli'ipa'ahana Kanaka'ole of Ka'ula, was a noted dancer, as was her mother, Nali'ipo'aimoku, who at the request of her beloved Queen Emma, traveled to Kaua'i, Ni'ihau, and Ka'u to dance, accompanied by her cousin, the noted chanter Kuluwaimaka. This occurred shortly after the death of Emma's husband, Kamehameha IV.

When just an infant, following Hawaiian tradition, I was given to my grandmother, Kawena, to be raised by her. Literally while I sat at her knee and listened, she immersed me in Hawaiian culture. Kawena had also been a *hanai*, raised by *her* grandmother Nali'ipo'aimoku.

The journey starts with the story of an *ipu heke,* a Hawaiian double-gourd hula instrument.

My grandfather, Napoleon Kaloliʻi Pukuʻi, made all hula implements for my grandmother, mother, and my aunt, Namaka, back in the 1930s and '40s.

My mother's *ipu* is an old Hawaiian gourd. These sound different from those used today that are imported from California and Mexico.

Mother kept her *ipu* in a decorated wooden box, where it had stayed unopened since she passed away almost 30 years ago. The box sat next to my dresser; clothes and some of my belongings were stacked on it.

A couple of years ago, I was awakened very early one morning with a strange urge—it was almost as if a voice was saying, *Open the box!*

I took the things off it and opened the box. The top of the *ipu heke,* the double gourd drum, was cracked and crumbling. I removed it carefully. The bottom was intact.

Going back to sleep was not even a thought. I discarded the broken pieces and stitching holding the two gourds together.

I looked in my shop storage area for an old garbage bag placed there about eight years earlier when my aunt/ foster mother, Namaka, Pat Bacon, gave me three of four raw *ipu.* Not having any immediate need, I'd bagged them and put them on a shelf.

Anyone who makes *ipu heke* knows that it is not easy to select two gourds that match well. Amazing—inside the old dusty bag was an *ipu* with the perfect size, shape, and color.

Everything else went "on hold" during the next two days as I cut, cleaned, and sewed the *po'o*—the head called *heke*—onto the bottom gourd.

I put my mom's cloth wrist band back on the *ipu*. I rubbed the *ipu* with *kukui* nut oil to moisturize it and produce a nice luster.

I struck it with my hand as a dancer or chanter would do.

It rang like a bell! The resonance filled the room.

The restored *ipu* was a reminder of my mother, the gifted hula dancer. I put it on a shelf in her honor.

A couple of shelves away sat my beloved grandmother Mary Kawena Puku'i's *ipu heke.*

Something had happened. But it would be years before I realized the meaning.

One of my greatest enjoyments is watching my six daughters dance together. They are all good dancers and began when very young.

They played with hula implements, rather than toys. Hula was in their bloodlines.

Kuhi is the youngest. Aloha Dalire, her *kumu,* decided it was time for her to represent her *halau,* Keolalaulani Halau Olapa O Laka, in the Miss Aloha Hula competition. It is for the very best from hula schools.

Ancestral Honor

Given her genealogy, Kuhi decided she would dedicate her performance to *kupuna,* her ancestors. She asked me for old family chants; I gave her a collection to choose for *kahiko,* the ancient hula presentation.

For her hula 'auwana, modern hula, Kuhi wanted to dance to something written by her great-grandmother, so many now are considered "classics."

She asked to look through an old, tattered spiral notebook grandmother gave me in the 1970s. She had written the words and translations for me to keep.

Kuhi came across "Kilauea," a *mele* created in the late 1940s or early 1950s, which had beautiful words but was not set to music. She kept returning to it. She knew this was the *mele* to which she wanted to dance.

Her *kumu* hula, Aloha Dalire, took the words to Kuhio Yim, Sean Pimentel, and Corey Oliveros. She wanted these young musician friends of hers to create and perform the melody. Kuhio, who spearheaded this effort, was more than a little nervous about creating a melody to go with the words, given the stature of the legendary author, Mary Kawena Puku'i!

Kuhio called Aloha, saying he was really having a hard time. "All I keep hearing in my head is old-style music."

Aloha said, "Well, then that's what it's supposed to be."

We heard it for the first time a few weeks before going to Hilo. Everyone loved it—much to the relief of the melody composer. It was simple, old-style. I'm sure Kuhio and his colleagues received help from beyond.

The three composer-musicians presented "Kilauea" beautifully at the competition. Joining them were Kuana Torres of Na Palapalai, singing the lead, and Keawe Lopes, UH Hawaiian language professor, playing the piano.

Because of the time it took to create the melody, and with so many preparations for the event, Kuhi didn't have a chance to practice with the musicians until the morning of the competition.

Although I didn't call attention to it, I realized it was significant that Kilauea was actively erupting. This new activity started months prior to and progressively intensified right up to the beginning of the annual Merrie Monarch Hula Competition.

Why did it have meaning to me? Our ancestral home is the district of Kaʻu and we claim Pele, the Fire Goddess, as our ancestor. As members of her Fire Clan, the bones of many generations of our family had been, in Hawaiian tradition, wrapped in tapa and, after proper preparation and ceremony, were tossed into Kilauea Crater for Pele to accept.

My grandmother told me that if Pele did not accept the remains as "family," the bundle would be thrown out of the crater.

She added, with pride, "None of our family were ever rejected."

This occurred from time immemorial. It was my grandmother's grandmother, Naliʻipoʻaimoku, who received the first Christian burial in our family.

Homeland

It was important to Kuhi that she visit those places mentioned in the chants and song she was going to dance to and she asked me if I would go with her to the Big Island for that purpose. So, at the end of January, Kuhi, her fiancé TC, and I flew to Hilo and met my very close friend, Kanaʻe Keawe and my daughter Pele, her husband Kekoa, and her children Kalamanamana, Leha, and

Naliʻipoʻaimoku. We spent the day taking Kuhi to all places mentioned in the chants and *mele*.

Our first stop was Hawaiʻi Volcanoes National Park. As we parked at Halemaʻumaʻu and proceeded to the lookout, a beautiful, bright rainbow appeared across the crater. Kuhi went to the edge and presented her *hoʻokupu*, her gift. I held her about her shoulders, both of us with tears in our eyes; it was all about returning home and being with our beloved Pele and those many ancestors whose bones were deposited there.

Kuhi didn't have to verbalize what she was feeling. I hugged her shoulder and whispered, "I know, I feel the same way." Our hearts were filled with thoughts of *ʻohana* and pure, unconditional aloha.

We spent the rest of the day visiting Kaʻu and the places where our *ʻohana* walked, fished, and raised their food and families. We went to Kalae, Mana, Unulau, Palahemo, where I had gazed at the water below while standing next to my beloved grandmother over 47 years earlier. We saw Ahukini, Waiʻohinu, Manakaʻa, Waikapuna, Iliʻili hanau, Pahala, Naʻalehu, and Haniumalu.

We had lunch at Waiʻohinu Park. I recalled traveling with my grandmother to those places as a youngster. I pointed out where Uncle Willie Meinecke's house was—we had stayed there for a few nights. A few houses down the road was Uncle George Kawaha's home—grandmother and I had visited with him.

Uncle George was a former sheriff of Kaʻu, not very big, but kind and with aloha. My grandmother had told me a story about him breaking up a fight on horseback, lifting two men, one in each hand, and riding, full gallop, to the jailhouse.

He was a *lua* practitioner and I recently heard more stories about him from others.

I was alone with my grandmother, those many years ago, when she received the call that George Kawaha had passed away. She cried on my shoulder for a long time. . . .

It was a trip that was important to Kuhi; it would help her to portray these places, now that she had visited them.

The Reason

Months earlier, after considering her options, Kuhi told me at home of her decision to do a sitting hula using an *ipu*. This is an old style seldom seen anymore called "hula *kuolo*." I suggested she try her grandmother's *ipu*. She said later she felt good using it.

One afternoon, I called her to tell her we should give it a name, since it had new life. She told me she planned to name the *ipu* Ke-Ahi-o-Pele (Pele's Fire) if it was okay with me? It surely was.

Uncle Ka'upena Wong, considered Hawai'i's premier chanter, was *ho'opa'a,* the chanter, for my mother when they performed together for many years. My grandmother was his teacher.

He told me that grandma said that the *ipu* was one's dance partner in the hula *kuolo*.

A couple of weeks before the competition, I was standing in my daughter Kawena's garage, talking to Kuhi, when this thought rushed to mind.

I said, "Kuhi, it was *your grandmother* who prompted me to get up that morning and take her *ipu* out of its wooden crate and repair it. She knew someone would have need of it. That someone, she just told me, *is you!*

Unseen Audience

Our entire *'ohana* flew to Hilo to be Kuhi's seen support group. There would also be the unseen, about whom I dreamed.

In my sleep, the night before her performance, I visualized our excited ancestors. Word had spread, they were scurrying around the stadium, seeking a perfect spot to watch Kuhi on stage. They took their places. In the front, center, was my grandmother; seated to her right was my mother; to my grandmother's left were her mother and grandmother.

My grandmother graciously invited her elders to sit in her prime spot. They said, "No, you sit there, Kawena." I saw endless rows of folks, eagerly awaiting her performances—they must all have been relatives and their friends.

Kuhi said nothing as I described this, but I knew she had understood and absorbed my words.

A few months before going to Hilo, Kuhi had asked if I would please accompany her on stage and carry her mat.

This was important to her. Of course, I agreed.

I went to the Edith Kanakaole Stadium early that evening to meet her.

Several girls from her *halau* were already there and talking excitedly about going to Halemaʻumaʻu that morning. Because Kilauea's activity had closed off areas to tourists, each *halau* was escorted, one-by-one, by park rangers.

The girls said that it was completely silent when they arrived, but as Kuhi chanted and presented her *hoʻokupu* for Pele, they heard rumblings. Smoke rising from the crater intensified.

Kuhi had asked me that morning about what gift should she bring. I said to take along a bottle of gin for Pele. It was what her grandmother, Pele's namesake, had always done.

Aloha later told me this story: "Before we went to the lookout, I was sitting on the wall in the parking lot, waiting for our turn, talking to Merrie Monarch broadcaster Paula Akana. We both looked at the rising smoke. I asked Paula if, as a child, she'd ever played the game of looking at the clouds and imagining formations.

"Then, almost instantly, in the smoke, Paula and I saw Aunty Io—Iolani Luahine, Hawaii's legendary dancer— with her hair up.

"We also saw images of Aunty Emma DeFries, a relative of ours, and my late sister, who had helped me with the *halau*.

"There was no question about who appeared," Aloha stated.

When it became Kuhi's turn, we all entered and, after placing Kuhi's mat down, I sat onstage behind her to watch her do her *oli* and then her hula *kuolo*.

I was entranced. I didn't know exactly what she was going to present because, not feeling well, I hadn't attended the *halau's ho'ike*, held for families to preview the *halau's* Merrie Monarch entries.

I was proud of the way she delivered her opening *oli,* "Ka Lawai'a Holona I Ke Kai O Manaka'a," about her ancestors, Kanaka'ole, his younger brother, Kekipio-O-Haililani, and a cousin, Kawelu, fishing in the sea at Manaka'a, Ka'u. It was composed about 1850.

Kuhi dances "Kilauea."

Kanakaʻole was a noted *kahuna laʻau lapaʻau,* a medicinal *kahuna,* as is mentioned in King Kalakaua's journal. He was also a *kahuna hoʻouluiʻa,* an expert on fish habits. Kanakaʻole was Kuhi's great-great-great grandfather.

Her language was flawless; many remarked that, even if they didn't understand, she obviously knew her language and chanted with such confidence. Kuhi won the Hawaiian Language Award, given by the Office of Hawaiian Affairs.

I had told Kuhi never to let anyone's judgment affect her. What she was doing was really between her and her ancestors. She should just tell the story as they would.

I watched her sway and caress her grandmother's *ipu* as she told the story of the beloved Kaʻu chief and relative, Kupakeʻe. I was transported to another time.

How magnificent! I thought to myself. I particularly loved the firm way she chanted the first line:

"Aʻole au i makemake ia Kona, O Kaʻu kaʻu." (I care not for Kona, for Kaʻu is mine!)

When she stood, chanted, and danced "Kiʻekiʻe Kaʻu Kua Makani," in tribute to our Kaʻu ancestors, I just sat in admiration of this young woman dancing in front of me for those in attendance and for countless others watching the live broadcast.

She performed for all who had danced and walked this *ʻaina,* this land before her. She honored them with pure and sincere aloha.

A few nights before her performance, I had asked our ancient *ʻohana* to inspire her and to place a *kihei pua* on her shoulders—figuratively, a shawl of flowers.

It was a splendid evening for this young woman who, with joy in her heart, and pure love for this art form called hula, danced and chanted in sincere tribute to her ancestors.

After being proclaimed Miss Aloha Hula, and as Kuhi was being congratulated by *'ohana* and friends on the stage, I talked with Kimo Kahoano, the Merrie Monarch commentator.

He kept saying that he felt the Merrie Monarch wasn't about competition, it was all about family. I wholeheartedly agreed.

I just didn't reveal just how large an intergenerational family we had there supporting Kuhi.

The legacy continues.

Postscript

I called George Naope at his home a day or two after last year's Merrie Monarch Festival (April 2009). Uncle George is the festival's cofounder. He was ill—his brother was screening visitors; I wanted to know if my wife and I could visit Uncle George.

"Come on up," he relayed through his brother.

I brought a surprise gift—a video featuring Ray Kinney with Uncle George chanting on it. He was then in his twenties.

How elated this made him!

At his bedside, we discussed Kuhi's performance at the Merrie Monarch Festival. Uncle George wanted to focus particularly on her hula *kuolo*.

Then he said, with a twinkle in his eyes:

Eh, nobody dance like that anymore!

George Naope passed away on October 26, 2009, at age 81 in Hilo, followed recently by fellow cofounder Dorothy "Auntie Dottie" Thompson, who left us on March 19, 2010, at age 88.

View Kuhi's performances: Kuhi's hula auwana, "Kilauea": http://www.kitv.com/video/15790188/index.html and Kuhi's hula kahiko: http://www.youtube.com/watch?v=JT6Vx47ESZY/

40.

Perfect Harmony

"How's it feel to be part of a hot new trend?" I asked 78-year-old George Kekoolani. It was 2008, and I'd just finished reading *Pitch Perfect*, a new book by Mickey Rapkin, *GQ*'s editor, about a cappella singing. Once a collegiate subculture with members as far afield as Cole Porter and Osama bin Laden, singing without instrumental accompaniment is a fast-growing phenomenon. There are more than 1,200 on-campus groups.

"Being in harmony has always been big in Hawaii," George replied in his crystal-clear tenor. He'd been with the Singing Men of Kamehameha for 53 years.

His memorial service was held in 2010 at the school chapel; fellow songsters performed. We sang to him in the hospital, and George mouthed the words to every song along with us. He'd been singing them over half a century. His daughter Tina danced a bedside hula.

A story is often behind Hawaii's good things such as "harmony." This one links German gemütlichkeit—

cheerful social acceptance—with Hawaiian aloha—sense of well-being.

King Lot's building program energized the kingdom and impressed visiting dignitaries. But his 12-man band embarrassed him. He wrote Germany's emperor a beseeching letter: "Please send me a bandmaster!"

"The Waltz King," Johann Strauss Jr., was in charge of German Army bands. He picked Heinrich "Henri" Berger for the Hawaii job, allowing him a five-year furlough. King Lot, last of the Kamehamehas, died six months after Berger arrived. Voters elected David Kalakaua as king.

"The Arions" greeted Berger at the boat. This male singing ensemble was composed of German immigrants who sang "Die Rose," Schubert's new song in five-part harmony (TTBBB) in one breath. (Schubert's is only 30 seconds long. Bette Midler, Oahu's Radford High School graduate, won a Tony Award for singing a longer and different "The Rose.")

Hawaiian music then consisted of a few missionary hymns. Berger fostered a musical explosion: He composed over 275 Hawaiian songs and wrote down every single Hawaiian melody he heard.

He wrote music to lyrics by King Kalakaua and "Hawai'i Pono'i" was born. Kalakaua's compositions reveal why he was called The Merry Monarch: "Koni Au" and "Ninipo" have a German Beer Garden sound. Liliuokalani, the king's sister, became a prolific and versatile composer with lieder-like melodies (sweet and artful).

In 1947, Charles E. King told me how Kamehameha School's a cappella singing tradition began.

"Teacher Theodore Richards was inspired by discovery of great musical talent among us boys in 1889. He gave us Hawaiian songs to sing in four-part harmony. He was able to get into the hearts of his pupils.

"He took us on concert tours around the islands, making us proud of ourselves, proud of our school, and making Hawaiian audiences proud of our accomplishments. He personally paid for our white tuxedos, white formal dress shirts and bow ties, white socks, and white patent leather shoes. Our parents wouldn't have been able to afford such grandeur, we certainly didn't have the money for it."

In 1893 new principal Richards immediately hired Henri Berger to develop and broaden Kamehameha's music program.

Kamehameha Schools Alumni Glee Club president Cliff Carpenter said, "Director Aaron Mahi keeps us versatile. We learn classical projection—real singing, unlike modern-day singers whose voice can't reach the front row without a microphone."

Mahi explains, "Male voices improve with age; rich mellowness doesn't develop until the late 30s." That's why George Kekoolani always sounded so amazing!

"I joined the Prince Kuhio Club's chorus to learn Hawaiian," said a former Canadian. "The leader invited me to direct a song for our Christmas Party. When I finished, she announced: 'Merry Christmas! This is now your group.'"

She's composed over 15 Hawaiian scores. Competing against other Hawaiian Clubs in song contests, similar to a German "Sangerfest"—remember "The Sound of Music?"—her group often wins with one of her own compositions.

Well-known for her large oil paintings of Hawaiian transformational and generational scenes, she is called "Leohone," a Hawaiian name:

The twenty-year-old Honolulu Men's Chorus sings choral versions of Hawaiian songs, Broadway music, and popular songs. Last year it performed Gabriel Faure's "Requiem Mass."

Simply by being, singers foster a sense of community. A member explained: "Through music, the gay, lesbian, bisexual, and transgender community—and its friends—have an avenue to participate in the heritage of our island home."

The Hawaii Youth Opera started nearly 50 years ago because local opera productions need a children's chorus.

Director Nola A. Nahulu says, "We foster personal social development and a lifetime of music appreciation for ages 5 to 18. Youngsters work in nine age segments. Na Leo Kuhoʻokahi, our mixed group, sings a cappella Hawaiian music.

Nahulu organized "Kane," a recent evening of male groups' singing. It opened in breathtaking fashion: Seventy-six young men grouped in quartets (TTBB) ringed Kawaiahaʻo Church's second-floor balcony.

Dressed in white formal wear, these Azusa Pacific University singers from California began the program with an eleventh-century plainsong—"Of the Father's love begotten, ere the worlds began to be." Blend and timbre were an unequaled experience.

Possibly apocryphal, this story reminds us that a bandleader from Germany created a profound difference in Hawaii's harmony and even in the sound of our words.

Berger's Germanic origins made it difficult for him to pronounce the soft "w" in Hawaiian and English as well. He'd say: *Velcome to Hah-vai-ee.*

Consequently, a hard "v" sound is ubiquitous in some Hawaiian words; e.g., the "w" in Hawaii is pronounced as "v."

41.

Oktoberfest

It was the last Saturday in September 1938 in Honolulu's Kapiolani Park. Brining, sauerkraut making, cheese making, pickling, and meat smoking had been going on for months.

I was just a little kid squeezed in tightly between Hans and Jerry, two big German guys, on the front seat in a black Ford pickup truck. We stopped at the Primo brewery to load the truck's cargo bed with kegs of beer, then drove to the icehouse for blocks of ice. Using ice picks, Hans and Jerry chopped ice into chunks to spread around the kegs. We were going after oysters and clams in Pearl Harbor's shallows.

After a couple of hours of this, Hans and Jerry layered the harvest around the beer kegs and spread chopped ice over oysters and clams and headed to the Oktoberfest.

Men at our Kapiolani Park picnic site eagerly unloaded the truck, tapped the kegs, sampled the beer, and called to the women to bring a mug and try some, because "It's chilled just perfectly!"

Everyone kept decorated steins close while shucking clams and creating wondrous things: stuffed clams, clam broth, clam chowder, horseradish-dressed raw clams, and raw oysters.

They put smaller clams in large pots, barely covering them with water, to "steam" open. They spread steamed clams on pans, took them to a table where everyone gathered around to dip clams in homemade butter, sprinkle on hot-pepper sauce, and gobble— between gulps of beer.

Folks began arriving with cheese, pickles, and the best of the wurst family—the pork, beef, and veal sausages called bockwurst, bratwurst, weinerwurst, weisswurst, and knockwurst.

The gang from Lihue, Kauai—"Germantown," as one person joking called it—brought hams, pigs' knuckles, *hendl* (chicken), sauerbraten, sauerkraut, and sour pickles.

Many were dressed for the occasion: women in colorful dirndl with puffed blouses, full skirts, and aprons. Men wore short-sleeved shirts and lederhosen—black or green leather shorts, not quite reaching their knees, held up by suspenders. They had on long socks and half boots. A cap with a bright feather topped the costume.

Men loaded grills with chunks of *kiawe* wood and started fires. When coals were red and glowing, they placed sausages on the grills to barbecue and sizzle.

Folks gathered around to drink beer; grilling meat aroma tantalized and excited appetites. Adults lifted and clinked mugs and sang the German equivalent of "For He's a Jolly Good Fellow":

Hoch soll sie leben, Hoch soll sie leben,

Hoch soll sie leben, Dreimal hoch!

Prosit! Down the hatch! Refill mugs, clink, slug down more beer, chomp sausage, converse excitedly about everything, repeat the drinking song. Continue the cycle—everyone's face grew ruddy.

Kids drank Spezi—German-style lemonade mixed with root beer—sweet and sour, a taste loved in Hawaii.

Ladies spread out the food on several tables. About two hundred of us were here; there must have been food for at least twice that many. You just don't know how good potato salad can be until you've had the vinegar-laced German style. It's true about their baked beans, too.

I won't even begin to describe the pastries—you might want to lick this page—strudel, cakes, and Austrian stuff to make you stuffed.

When everyone was satiated, an accordionist began playing. Singing joyfully, the crowd bounced up and down on the park grounds, dancing, twirling, sweating, and laughing. Two other musicians arrived: a big man with a baritone horn and his trumpet-playing wife, then along came a bass drummer.

While the musicians paused, men and women sang a four-word song: "Ein Prosit der Gemütlichkeit"—"Drink and to All Good Cheer," waving their mugs while singing. They sang it four times or so; everyone raised their mugs during the last Gemütlichkeit and finished with a hearty drink. A nice thing about all the dancing was that it made room for more food.

Intermittently, during the afternoon and into the evening, someone broke out into that song—of course the crowd joined in and helped to complete the ritual—capping it off with the cheerfully shouted *Prosit!*

I learned that Hawaii's German tradition is deep and rich; Henri Berger integrated Austrian and German melodies into Hawaiian music. In 1892 British and German Clubs merged to become the Pacific Club. George F. Straub founded Straub Clinic and Hospital in the early 1900s. Street names recall activities of early German families: Isenberg, Spreckels, Von Hamm Place, Hausten Street, and more.

I came to the party to see my friend Luther Aungst; he founded the telephone company in Kona and had a talking mynah named Birdie. "Sorry I couldn't bring Birdie," he said. "Birdie's lovelorn and lonely and might fly away with the park's mynahs. Then who'd talk with me?"

Mr. Aungst had the most amazing hobby. He kept a seismograph in his house and monitored volcanic activity. When learning of lava flows on the Big Island, he took some of the current year's silver dollars, went to the flow, twisted a forked stick into molten lava, put the lava on the ground and placed a silver dollar in it. Mr. Aungst has a huge collection of silver dollars encased in lava because the volcano erupted so often.

All of this happened in "Old-Time Hawaii," before the war, when being German during Oktoberfest—or just pretending to be—was loads of fun and fattening. Hardworking people didn't worry about calories then.

Homecoming

Ruth Vargo read the above story. Dick Case, *Syracuse Post Standard* columnist, describes what happened next.

* * *

A Syracuse meat market that specializes in German food is providing a modest banquet of goodies for a party for a U.S. serviceman who just got back from a tour of Iraq. The welcome home party's in Hawaii.

The supplier is Liehs and Steigerwald, the German shop on Grant Boulevard opened in 1936 by Ludwig Steigerwald. It now has a branch store in Clay.

The connection to the homecoming soldier—Jeffrey Lynn Vargo II of the 25th Infantry Division—is a former Syracusan and native of Hawaii, J. Arthur Rath. Arthur ran a Syracuse advertising agency of that name for years. He's retired to Hawaii and writes free-lance articles for the Hawaii Reporter newspaper.

Jeffrey's wife, Ruth, who is also in the Army, read an article by Arthur in the Reporter about a party with German food in Honolulu in 1938, when the writer was a child. Ruth contacted Arthur because his story gave her an idea for a party. Her husband is a fan of German chow and misses it.

Did Arthur know where she could find German makings in Hawaii?

In Syracuse, of course.

Chuck Madonna is one of the Liehs and Steigerwald's owners. He runs the Syracuse store. His partner is Jeff Steigerwald, who handles things at the north shop. Both are "special places," according to the proprietors.

Chuck tells me the order for Hawaii is going the farthest for perishable goods in the store's history. He's done orders for Afghanistan and Iraq but those were dry goods.

The butcher said he plans to mail knockwurst, bratwurst and bockworst as well as sauerkraut and German potato salad from Syracuse Tuesday night by UPS. The 30-pound package will be frozen and packed in Styrofoam and freezer packs.

"It should get there by Wednesday night," according to Chuck.

* * *

Dick Case writes human interest stories tied to his newspaper's area, as the late Bob Kraus did for the *Honolulu Advertiser.*

42.

Italian Table Life

An e-mail covered my cumulative shortcomings:

"This publication is 'Hawaii Reporter,' not '*Hawaiian Reporter*,'" was the grumble. You've been culturally narrow, ignoring all of us whose names end in a vowel.

"How about a slice of Italian life?"

I gulped, then replied:

"I write about those I know. Privileged to have associated with people culturally such as you, I'll present a bill of fare having appeal to every Italian gourmand out there."

Here it is.

From life experience within many cultures—Polynesian, Chinese, Japanese, Eastern and Western European, English, and Italian—I have found no families as food oriented as are traditional Italians. None! It is not just the food that's important, it is what it relates to in rituals (even though eels for Christmas Eve may not be included today because of squeamish Americanized youngsters, and the same holds true for the traditional Easter lamb's head).

Gathering together as a family unit is what makes mealtime important in Italian culture, as well as in others.

For Italians, mealtimes, usually a Sunday afternoon dinner, can be a *festa della famiglia* (family festival). These are the moments when they share their culture and eat it too. The leisurely meal allows time for father to impart wisdom and encourage give and take among people mattering the most to him.

Everyday Italians did without meat for a long time in their culture and found outstanding ways to make soups, sauces, and to create vegetarian meals. *Magro* (no meat) was believed to purify the body. Feasts and special occasions were some of the few opportunities to eat *grasso* (meat and rich foods). For everyday meals in many homes, pasta may be served as an appetizer. The sauce is exquisite but sparing, and other courses follow; the meal is finished with salad and then fruit.

In between the pasta and fruit, there may be one-dish meals such as spareribs, sausages, potatoes, and vegetables, broccoli-flavored polenta layered with sausages and cheese; pasta in the style of southern Italy with tomatoes, black olives, hot peppers, garlic, anchovies; and fine flat noodles or spaghetti; vegetarian lasagna, or perhaps beans and greens.

Full-course meals might include the following:

- Pumpkin gnocchi with shavings of smoked mozzarella and sage leaves; herb-scented roast turkey; salad of arugula and other greens; creamy vanilla-scented cheesecake;

- Or, vegetable soup with ribbons of sweet peppers; polenta (a thick mush of cornmeal) with pork; tiny sweet and sour onions; buckwheat flour cake with jam filling;
- Or, artichoke soup, chicken and risotto (a form of rice) flavored with balsamic vinegar; green salad and crunchy crusted bread; almond sponge cake served with mascarpone sauce (triple-cream cheese—tiramisu is an example);
- Or, creamy pumpkin-flavored rice, garlic and rosemary-studded leg of lamb; little croquettes in the shape of a fish; lemon granita and chocolate-hazelnut cookies.

Add to these hundreds of other possibilities, many specifically regional. Saints have their feast day and dishes that go with it, including varieties of desserts in abundance.

Eating festive foods has more meaning than just enjoying ritual soups and sweets from the past. It is a way of assimilating wisdom and something to be preserved. Italians' love for variety has helped make meals more interesting and healthy for many Americans.

There is a difference in how cultures interpret the proverbial "land of milk and honey."

An American folk song of the Great Depression describes "The Big Rock Candy Mountains":

With the birds and the bees and the cigarette trees, the lemonade springs where the whang doodle sings, and the soda water fountains. There's a lake of stew and of whiskey too, and the little streams of alcohol come trickling down the rocks.

Stew would only be a starter for Italians. In the *Decameron*, Giovanni Boccaccio (1313–1375) describes what Italians would expect in Paradise:

Where they tie up the vineyards with sausages, where you get a goose for a penny and a gosling thrown in for good measure.

Where there is a mountain made entirely of Parmesan cheese upon which lived people who did nothing but make macaroni and ravioli, which they cook in capon broth and later toss off the mountain, and whoever picks up more gets the most.

Nearby flows a stream of dry white wine, the best you ever drank, without a drop of water in it.

Luscious Italian meals aren't limited to home cooking here in cosmopolitan Hawaii. I enjoy them at Chez Pasta downtown and Verbano's in Aiea. Riffle through the telephone book's Yellow Pages, and you'll find many options. *Mangaro!*

43.

Missionary Cousins

A lush green oasis in the heart of downtown Honolulu provides public inspiration, nourishment, education, and a setting for special occasions. Stop by for breakfast or lunch, and step into a nineteenth-century atmosphere binding the past with the present.

"Public programming is our true purpose for existing," the Hawaiian Mission Children's Society president stated at the group's annual meeting on the grounds of its early 1800s buildings at 553 South King Street.

This meeting occurs on an April Saturday, close to the 1820 date when first pioneer missionaries arrived in Honolulu from New England. Descendents, referring to each other as "Cousin," gather to see how each other is doing and to sing traditional songs that lift their hearts. The only thing comparable is eastern college alumni reunions. Cousins resemble easterners—not surprising, considering the gene stock.

Ceremonies for the 157th Annual Meeting began with a prayer from the *kahu*, pastor of neighboring

Kawaiaha'o church. Many of Hawaii's original missionaries rest in its graveyard; they're sometimes visited during the day. Reports and elections of new officers were preludes to "The Competition."

Excitement rose under the tent as time for that approached. People looked around bright-eyed, smiled, and nodded to each other.

A Cousin stepped forward, rang a sailing ship's bell, and hollered:

"Roll Call."

Authoritatively, he declared: "The *Thaddeus,* the first ship to carry missionaries to Hawaii in April 14, 1820. . . ."

As he read names of the missionaries who'd been on board, their descendents stood to be counted.

This ritual was repeated for successive ships.

He announced the oldest descendant who was present: This 98-year-old lady waved cheerfully from a wheelchair.

He identified the youngest Cousin: A sleeping babe in arms.

He announced the name of this year's "Winning Family" that had 16 members present!

Roll Call Competition is keen. Seventy-seven is the largest-ever family showing; they came in 1941 to celebrate the centennial of their ancestor's arrival.

While we stood in the café's lunch line, a woman up front exulted to companions, "We won!" They beamed back.

Several persons represented four families of missionary stock. Hawaii's missionaries weren't real "Cousins" and intermarried. The bonding term descendents use with each other was derived much later.

"Singing" is the most emotional part of the annual gathering. Three songs always included in Hawaii's Cousin Society rituals express missionary zeal, concern for each other, and development of Hawaii into becoming missionaries' beloved homeland. (A real cousin says it's an affinity that's crept up during the past 180 years.)

Zealots

The "Second Great Religious Awakening" occurred when Hawaii's prospective missionaries were at highly impressionable ages.

One of America's most successful revivalists, young Charles Grandison Finney, attended what became upstate New York's Hamilton College. He declared that Christ's death satisfied public justice rather than retributive justice.

Finney's understanding of the atonement was that it opened the way for God to pardon people of their sin. He proposed "disjunction," a concept acquiring vitality in romantic literature: The heart versus the head, emotion versus intellect. This was quite a contrast to stern Calvinism zeal. After 1830, that approach became applied in Hawaii.

Finney's most controversial new measures were public praying of women in mixed-sex audiences, use of colloquial language, praying for people by name, and immediate church membership for converts.

Hawaii's missionaries, primarily idealistic young people, weren't all ministers.

My great-great-grandmother Sarah Joiner of Royalton, Vermont, heard Finney preach in Boston. Stirred by his enthusiastic religion and revivalism, she immediately decided to become a missionary. She'd gone to the meeting with Henry Lyman and needed a husband—the missionary society wanted only married couples.

Henry suggested his brother David Belden Lyman, who wanted to be a missionary to Indians in western New York.

David and Sarah quickly married. The Mission Board decided they should bring God to Hawaiians, and they left Boston on an almost six-month voyage, arriving in Honolulu in 1830 and ending in Hilo. They established a boarding school to provide book learning and manual arts training. Hilo's Lyman Museum and Mission House commemorates their work (www.lymanmuseum.org).

Young people were inspired both by Finney and the era's fervent songs. The drive "to convert" is reflected in Reginald Heber's hymn written in 1819, sung yearly at Cousins Society's reunions:

From Greenland's Ice Mountains
From India's Coral Strand,
From many an ancient River
From many a palmy plain,
They call us to deliver
Their land from error's chain.

Heber also wrote lyrics to the most widely recognized hymn of the last 150 years: "Holy, Holy, Holy."

The idealistic, world-saving inspiration Heber expressed rose again to a fervor in 1961 when John F. Kennedy called on Americans to enlist in the Peace Corps as a nonmilitary response to Chinese and Soviet Communistic thrusts into the Third World.

Cousins sing "Blest Be the Tie That Binds"; words are by John Fawcett (1782), music is by Hans Naegeli. Thought of as "Hawaii missionaries' theme song," it expresses love and concern for each other.

We finished our annual meeting with the song "Hawai'i Aloha" ("Beloved Hawai'i"); the words were written by the Big Island's Rev. Lorenzo Lyons (1859) to the melody of the Scottish hymn, "I Left It All with Jesus."

"Hawai'i Aloha" expresses allegiance to Hawaii as our earthly home.

Classmate Carl Wheeler and I, with ties to Finney's old school, wanted to share our perspectives with Mission House staff. We said:

"Your nineteenth-century frame building, shipped around Cape Horn during grass shack days, resembles many wooden houses of that period still used in Upstate New York. Destructive termites don't stand a chance there because of freezing winters. Some built in the eighteenth century are still occupied.

"Masts for sailing ships were grown in West Winfield, near our college.

"About 25% of missionaries traveling to Hawaii 'before the mast' came from central New York (1820–1865). In David Lyman's journal, the sailing ship ride from New England to Hawaii was 'harrowing.'"

I began proselytizing and personalizing; it's in my genes:

"Hearing Finney's preaching zeal inspired my ancestors to become missionaries; their original ideas went beyond Hawaii. Hilo Boarding School was the forerunner of Tuskegee and Hampton Institute, pioneer colleges for black Americans.

"During a period when higher education was white-male dominated, Finney became president of Oberlin College in Ohio, the first co-ed college. Under Finney it accepted black Americans as well."

"Elisha Loomis, another Finney convert from upstate New York, used books published on the press he brought with him from Rushville. Missionaries helped Hawaiians achieve the world's highest literacy rate."

Wheeler is from Geneva, New York, where Titus Coan attended the same medical school as did Elizabeth Blackwell, who was America's first woman doctor. Finney urged Coan to become a missionary and heal souls instead. He eventually administered to 15,000 Hawaiians.

During his career at Honolulu's private Mid-Pacific Institute, Wheeler gained national recognition as one of America's most distinguished mathematics instructors. He is a volunteer tutor at Kapiolani Community College.

The Hawaiian Mission Society is a welcoming interesting place, and the café's food will make you feel sprightly.

Hawaiian Mission Children's Society's varied public programming includes walking tours of Hawaii's Capital Cultural District, a printing press demonstration, and special exhibits. Noon lectures are held the first Tuesday of every month (bring lunch or pick up something at the museum's café). On-site programs, which range within preschool to grade eight, meet Hawaii State Standards for Social Studies.

Outreach programs include a costumed educator who introduces aspects of the early nineteenth century and presents hands-on activities. Find out what's happening on the website: *http://www.missionhouses.org*.

44.

Parade Patois

Mother mailed me King Kamehameha Day Parade commentary she heard from a woman sitting alongside her. The cheerful parade watcher spoke the ordinary language many of us grow up using—it's picturesque, entertaining, spirited, and right to the point.

Speaking Pidgin shows you're "local." Helping students overcome Pidgin English is a mighty challenge to educators because *it is so much fun!*

It is patois—a local dialect. I lived in New York where even neighborhoods have distinctive speaking styles. Remember how Leonard Bernstein and Steven Sondheim made inner-city kids' raunchy patois sound so entertaining in *West Side Story?*

Here's the slice of life that my mother, Hualani, shared.

* * *

My neighbor, a huge Hawaiian woman, made people move from the places at the curb alongside King Street in front of the library to give me a front seat because of my age.

When her friends, equally large women, arrived, I understood why she held such a broad area of the elevated curb as "her reserved seats."

She made steady commentary throughout the parade. The lieutenant governor rode by in a car, and she called out:

"You no business inside the car. You one young man, you walk!"

The ladies of the Kaahumanu Society came by in their black velvet clothes, wearing hats with yellow velvet lei:

"Hey sistah, your feet no sore, you wear the high heels for show off?"

To others parading by: "You think you high class you wear them gloves? You no hot you wear the velvet for show off?"

To other elegantly dressed-up women: "Where you gloves for make nice?"

To marching men dressed in black, representing the Kamehameha Order, she said:

"Why you fellows no choose nice ladies, nice clothes for walk you?"

Musicians or dancers took a breather while passing by, and she yelled in a loud voice:

"Play for us . . . dance for us. . . . You tired? Us tired, too. We wait one l-o-n-g time to come find this place to see you. Per-form!"

To Judge Richardson riding in a top-down convertible:

"Hey you William, where your horse? How come you no ride one? Your horse run away?"

As people stood in front of me, she loudly scolded them for blocking my view; if they didn't move she took action. She announced loudly:

"Get away! Why you no come last night *kapu* the same. Us stay here long time for to see."

To a stubborn Chinese man who shoved his way in front of me, she yelled:

"Go way! We no come to see your ugly Pake *okole*."* That made him move.

When the parade was over, I saw her on the grounds of Kawaiahao Church where Hawaiian food was being sold. She regreeted me:

"Hey sistah, you come *kau kau*. 'Cause you hungry, too?" Then she helped make room for me in the front of the food line.

* * *

This is our dialect; innovators at Bamboo Ridge Press (bambooridgepress.com) have successfully advanced its literary value. Don't you agree it is fun?

*I'm sure that parade interlocutor had used a crude one-syllable attention-grabbing word in English instead of Hawaiian *"okole."* Mother wouldn't put *that kind* of language in the mail to me.

45.

Beeswax and Other Symbols

I watched a relative prepare candles for a Mass in Honolulu's St. Andrews Cathedral and commented, "Do you know the significance of those beeswax candles? Friends of mine make them."

When she said "No," I realized others might also be in the dark. I wrote an explanation for Cathedral Candle Company, church candle makers, to place in each box of beeswax candles so volunteer altar guilders would know.

Symbolism affects our lives.

It certainly influenced Kamehameha IV and his consort Queen Emma. During a visit, they were impressed with the Church of England's panoply—contrasted to plain vanilla New England missionary religion. They asked for English help in making the Official Church of Hawaii "Episcopalian." Hence, St. Andrew's Cathedral, established 1862 with Hawaii's king and queen as its first communicants.

Some persons like to point out that "English Episcopalians had *an invitation* from the king and queen to bring their religion to Hawaii. They didn't just show up as American Calvinists did."

One-upmanship of high over low church is a way to describe that; New-Age Pentecostals don't care.

The mid-1800s was an especially exciting time in the religious field, and it's no wonder that our young king and queen were impressed by what they saw in England. Christian mysticism was reawakening. After 300 years, the Puritan mania for barren interiors and lack of ritual and symbolism had waned and the inner meaning of the liturgy was being made known to all people.

Church music was being revived in its ancient original beauty. Old Christmas carols came out of hiding; composers created new ones. Candles were back on altars and being used in traditional ways.

During the onslaught of reformists, German monasteries had protected examples of once-flourishing Middle Ages religious symbolism. They brought them out of caves and shared their meanings. Jacob Steigerwald, a young Bavarian candle designer under this *einfluss* (influence), came to Syracuse, New York, America's candle-making center.

European immigrants were flowing into an America that was becoming industrialized. This created a tremendous growth in Catholicism. Four generations later, the Steigerwalds continue producing only church candles—"the living flame"—symbolizing the Son of God.

Along with traditional candles, Jacob's great-grandsons have introduced high-relief sculptured candles with translucent overlays creating beautiful tonal effects.

I describe them today as "the Michelangelos of candle making!"

Beeswax is a religious symbol, a beautiful and poetic expression of a thought, an eye-word appealing to mind and heart by its wealth of meaning.

Symbols are used to express abstract ideas. For instance, a ring is love that has no end (circle being emblematic of the idea of eternity). The *Trinity* is shown by the triangle or interwoven circles.

Gold is used at any time of the church year to represent victory, joy, and eternal life. *White* is a joyous liturgical color representing eternal life and light. *Green* stands for growth, life, hope, and victory. *Red* signifies fire, love, and sacrifice. *Blue* represents faith or trust. *Violet* (combination of red and blue) is the color of remorse, repentance, and preparation. The *anchor* means the cross, a symbol of safety for the navigator on the stormy sea of life.

The church is said to be a candlestick, holding aloft a burning candle because "The Son of God is the light of the world."

I suggested that the Stiegerwalds place a card in each box of beeswax altar candles with this information:

"True to the tenets of early Christian ages, the light these beeswax candles bring to a church signifies the presence of Christ. The human nature of Christ is symbolized by the purest form of beeswax produced from the bodies of virgin bees used to nourish each candle's flame, making the flame proper in size and consistent, long-burning of unchanging color. The lighting of them expresses the spiritual meaning: Your light comes, and the splendor of the Lord goes over you."

Cathedrals' designs are based on ancient studies of liturgy executed with graphic sophistication and fresh-looking colors.

Young people are very symbol conscious—just look at the logos, brand, and team names emblazoned on their clothes and caps. The role of products associated with ritual is to help put everyone in the frame of mind for which symbolism is intended.

46.

Chinese Pioneers

Over 150 persons expressed veneration to their ancestors in Kaimuki's Kilauea Recreation Center. Even two large, fierce creatures became cowed lions, awed by the majesty of the occasion. Beating drums spurred them to perform jauntily just as ceremonial Chinese lions should.

Center of attention was Ken Yee, who, with his late wife Nancy Wong Yee, the Hawai'i Chinese History Center, and 65 families, recounted moving stories of *Chinese Pioneer Families of Maui, Molokai, and Lanai.*

This 400-plus-page book, 25 years in the making, encompasses 220 years of comprehensive personal and Island history that never seems to wander.

The recounting begins with a nineteenth-century exodus to Hawaii, mainly from villages in the Pearl River Delta, the region now known as Guangdong. Family stories are organized by regions; for example, West Maui, Lahaina, and Wailuku.

This structure and masterful editing reinforces impressions of just what life "was like" in each region.

You gain a feel for each community and its people. All is sensitively done to help readers learn about personalities. For example:

"Papa's dry goods store was located in the hub of Maui business. The Caucasian influence in business was strong and pervasive for Papa and he developed an intense interest in the Wall Street Stock Market Exchange. He invested heavily in stocks of companies listed on the exchange. He became increasingly westernized in appearance. As a debonair young businessman, he dressed well in American-tailored suits, sported a Panama hat, and drove a Ford touring car.

"This, however, did not affect his profound belief in the Taoist philosophy, Confucianism, and the significance of Chinese traditions and customs. He accessorized his outfit with a jade tie pin and a heavy 24-carat gold chain with two carved jades in his lapel—typical Chinese symbols for double assurance of good health and prosperity. He taught his family that symbols confer the virtues of good omens and represent the whole of Chinese philosophy, an essential part of Chinese culture."

The audience was thrilled by a costumed ensemble providing the renowned Chinese art of drumming and percussion performance.

Musicians performed on powerful thunder drums. All could feel the intense sound. The two dancing lions focused on Ken Yee and his daughter Sylvia Yee. The Yees tantalized the lions—holding *li see* offerings hanging from sticks seemingly close, then snatching them out of reach until the dancing was over.

A cased exhibit honored Dr. Sun Yat-sen, first president of the Republic of China. It illustrated, as the new book explains, some of the influence Chinese in Hawaii had on the political ideas and history of modern China.

Dr. Sun Yat-sen graduated from Iolani Episcopal Boys School in 1882 and was issued a Territory of Hawaii birth certificate.

If, as Governor Lingle suggests, China represents new economic opportunities for Hawaii's lagging economy, more of us need to know about those who came here more than two centuries ago and how profound Chinese influence became.

I tagged along because of one of my ancestors is mentioned in the book. It states, "The first sugar mill on Maui was built in 1828 by Hungtai, a partnership of Ahung and Atai."

Great-Great Grandfather Ahung, a *tong see,* or sugar maker, sold white sugar made at his mill in his store, Hungtai, on the corner of Fort and Merchant Streets. He could do brown sugar, too, but you could sell white for a premium. He was one canny Chinaman. G-G-Grandfather also had a restaurant (of course) and a hotel that served as a community center and businessmen's meeting place.

I've written elsewhere about how a dense crowd, including his bar friends and a band, followed Atai's body—my ancestor's partner—to the Protestant Cemetery where he was buried. The band cheerfully performed on the pipe, cornet, and drum while Atai's many houris (girlfriends) wailed.

Atai's Chinese countrymen had their own musical group, and it performed Chinese opera music for the ceremony. Drumming at the Kilauea Recreation Center made me reflect on the Chinese sounds of music:

Ee-e-e, yih! Bong!
Clat-a-clat-a-clat and a Bong!
Slamming on a gong,
Beating with a stick,
In a shrill falsetto,
Like the scratch of a pin,
Scraping on a cat-gut nerve.
Ee-e-e—yih! Bong!

Did you know that Chinese opera is among the world's oldest dramatic art forms? Now that the governor has traveled for us, I will sensitize my Occidental ears and eyes and join others in welcoming Chinese tourists' who'll contribute to Hawaii's economic resuscitation. That's what folks in the Yee's new book did over 200 years ago.

Celebrities

Our minds preserve thoughts
about precious persons.
These are some who added distinctive flavor
And their personal zest to life in Hawaii.

47.

Renaissance Men: Quack, Kui, Face

We four 12-year-old boarding students became lifelong friends. All entered creative fields. Kui left shockingly soon, at age 34.

The other two exceeded the biblical "Threescore years and ten" (Psalm 90:10).

I write this paean describing their lasting influence on Hawaii.

Birth anniversaries for Kui (7/14) and Don (8/13) astrologically identify them as Leos. Both were stereotypically so.

George (10/17), a Libra, shone so brightly like the Sun.

I'm a Capricorn, an "Old Goat"—easily discernable.

While reflecting on that triumvirate, the melody of "Only Remembered," an old-time gospel hymn the four of us sang in school, flows through my head. I mouth the words: "Only remembered . . . by what they have done."

. . . Don Ho, we called him "Quack,"
Strode forward determinedly like a duck.
Born leader, we followed, trusting his pluck.

. . . "Kui," Lee's moniker,
Means "string together such as lei flowers."
His wreaths of songs capture fleeting hours.

. . . George Kanahele, "Face,"
Serious youth with an adult visage,
Foresaw true success—not a vague mirage.

While many Hawaiians deserve a cheer,
These, our inspirers, I personally hold dear—
"Lion-singers" Kui Lee and Don Ho:
Our old-time cheer: *Hana Hou!* Way to Go!

Renaissance men, who awakened our life,
Overcame inborn shame, languor, and strife:
Through them, "Hawaiian," once not fashionable,
Now means "identity, pride, capable."

Here's how it started by three young men fine,
Who'd known each other since boarding-school time:

. . . Don serves beer in Honey's, mother's small dive,
Organ behind bar keeps his mind alive.

He's shy, plays chang-a-lang chords—no big thing,
Working men come there to drink, not to sing.
In arrives Kui, skinny little elf,
Says he left New York because of ill health.

Quickly offers lots of pushy advice,
His orders are "New Yorkie," not real nice:
"Put organ up front, song melodies play,
Urge all to join in, singing it their way.
"Singing will make drinkers feel a real high.
Invite school songster pals and Marlene Sai,
Your business will become okie dokie;
Honey's then will predate Karaoke."

Don Ho's music—huge hit in the country,
But packed crowds in small bar not real comfy.
Waikiki nightclub Duke's sliding downhill—
With a kiss Duke and Don, seal a big deal.

It was then that the Renaissance began:
Courage and talent from a special man—
The sixties, with Don behind an organ,
Hawaii he loves changing around him,
Playing, singing in his smooth baritone,
Showman talk, literate Pidgin well honed.

Treats touchy subjects, never judgmental:
Just the facts of life now fundamental
About surging high-rise economy,
Disappearing Diamond Head, land, and sea,
Influx of relocating millionaires,
Beaches blocked, locals can't go anywheres.

Don won't sigh "Auwe" throughout his live show;
Hawaii's changing, it's what we all know,
He can relate this through current events.
Taking you inside doors, windows, and vents.

Fusing local music with Mainland Pop,
Singing the song Kui wrote: "Suck 'Em Up,"
Raising mai tai glasses with its logos
Then people don't drink, *they drank!* at Ho's show.

Now once everyone's feeling real mellow,
Ho demonstrates being a grand fellow:
Acknowledges R&R guys from Vietnam.
"Newly married? Stand. Give them a big hand.
Return visitors? How many times now?
And you know every song I sing? Oh, wow!

"Would you like to sing your state's song, soldier?
Band—Start it loud, until he gets bolder.
Grandmas, we'll talk when we're *pau* with the show,
You are my favorite people you know."

After Ho finishes amenities,
Flattering guest artists in "their best keys,"
He instills Hawaiian pride with his jokes,
Verbalizing stuff felt by older folks.
Explains words and feelings in his songs so
Grandparents' thoughts come through from years ago.
You know that their old-time magic is real
By how Ho conveys the things he will feel.

. . . Kui's linkages advanced life a lot,
Fused local music with his main-stream pop.
After years on stage in New York City
Lee believed in drama—not being "pretty."
Used psychological affirmation,
And anti-establishment rebellion.

Don's voice, backed by Alii's harmony,
Leads a hip new state, not territory.
Kui wrote music making a statement,
His time being short made him impatient.
Tosses his Maui song into beach trash,
"Won't go anywhere, I wrote it too fast."
His wife pulls it out and gives it to Ho:
"Lahainaluna"—that song we all know.

Overcome by cancer, not feeling fit,
Writes "I'll Remember You," Don's biggest hit.
Kui left us when he was thirty-four,
Ho's voice helped project his fame evermore.

. . . George grew up poor, with the touch of Midas.
"Acres of Diamonds? All here around us."
During his PhD program at Cornell
Called "The Little Engine that Really Will."
His mind's so refined, most others can't see
How he can explain things so logically.

Simple Plain English, and very clearly.
Making state government people wary,
Political appointees become chary.
He gives answers for problems that they fear:
Like creating tourism edges here.

He wanted to involve Hawaiian lore,
Making Waikiki more than a big store,
140 ideas to improve its face,
Gives locals, tourists, something to embrace.

He fosters attitude changes as well:
"Adding Hawaiian values would be swell."
Each proposal is backed by a study,
Success with income growing steady.
Prophets don't have honor in their hometown,
Since that's true, George went elsewhere for renown.

George's wise choices for moderation
Doesn't fit with local agitation.
UH protestors roar: "Changes now—see!"
Stoned blank faces exult: "Maui Wowie!"
Rebels have no cause? "Then let's make one up!"
Their argot slurs into "Hey pal, Wassup?"

Confronters with signs and T-shirts make scenes,
One lands in Congress, has governor dreams.
Those waves became puddles, Ho didn't slow,
George's dictum lasts: "It's better to know."
His wisdom remains in important books,
Inspiring discerning taking close looks.
His Hawaiian studies are seminal,
Groups that he fostered may be eternal.
George died a week after his first sky dive,
Heart attack, while helping Guam natives thrive.

Don's messages came in Hawaiian style,
Delivered with class, charm, and winning guile.
George helped us reflect on what's here that's good:
Being distinctive, his number-one "should."

Kui's music makes you feel nostalgic,
Wise and tuned in, not melodramatic.
Quack and Face, each my boarding-school roommate,
From youth throughout adulthood we would relate.
The third, my pal, pixie dust in his brain,
Created magic, helped broaden Ho's fame.

Growing older has improved my vision;
Seeing the truth now with realism
I know those three boys growing into men
Helped make Hawaii's Renaissance: Amen!

48.

Duke: Fastest Thing in Water

Everyone growing up here in the twentieth century knew of Duke Kahanamoku. Since Duke served as sheriff of Honolulu for 13 consecutive terms, most persons quickly explained *just how* they knew him.

Even before becoming Honolulu's Official Greeter, he was a personal symbol of what was best of 'Being Hawaiian.'

Everyone knows of his swimming fame as an Olympian: He won five Olympic medals in swimming from 1912 to 1924.

The Swimming Hall of Fame also recognizes how he popularized the crawl stroke and what was then a new way of kicking that crawlers still use.

He is known for being the "Father of Surfing" and for popularizing it here after it waned during Missionary Days. They discouraged such frivolity. He helped to make surfing a worldwide sport by introducing it to California and Australia.

Being a former eastern sculler, I'm eager to give you this little-known insight on the most versatile aquatic athlete of all time:

Duke Kahanamoku was Hawaii's sculling and sweep-rowing champion!

Kahanamoku rowed when Regatta Day was Hawaii's major sporting event. King Kalakaua's birthday on November 16 was observed with a yearly Regatta Day.

Back then, Honolulu Harbor presented an animated appearance. Wharves were crowded with spectators, and sailing vessels were decorated with bunting. But over and above all was the display of humanity on every yard and spar; the long line of masts and yards was thick with boys and men. (I'm not being provincial; of course there were loads of women spectators, but they wore dresses and didn't crawl up on the masts.)

This was when sailing vessels, such as the *Falls of Clyde*, were the prime means of transportation to and from Hawaii.

Duke loved rowing. It was the only sport in which he could really hear and feel the crowd's excitement. You can't do that when your head is underwater or you are beyond the reef on a board.

It looked effortless for him; he was so steady. He drove his legs hard, like a breaststroke kick, moved his arms in a rhythm similar to when he was paddling a surfboard a great distance. That's how one sculls.

At Regatta Day in 1917, Duke defeated his nearest rival in the senior sculls race by five boat lengths.

The big event, as always, was the senior six, a two-mile race.

According to the *Honolulu Star-Bulletin*, wagers were as much as $1,000 for the winner between the Healani

Blue, champions for the past seven years, and the Hilo team.

It was when a dollar had big value.

The Myrtle Reds, with Duke as stroke, were rowing a new boat for the first time. They weren't considered in the running. Myrtle members voted to name the boat after Kahanamoku, the newspaper wrote, "Inasmuch as the Duke is the fastest thing in the water."

It described the race: "Duke's shining bronze body stood out from the rest as the sun glistened on it. He wore a sailor hat, by now one of his trademarks.

"In a very close race, Duke pushed his crew to finish first with several hard strokes, just ahead of Hilo.

"It reminded spectators of the way Duke finished his swimming races; he always paced himself and kept enough energy in reserve to win."

Back then, spectacular 14-oared double-banked cutters raced. King Kalakaua, his sister Princess Liliuokalani, and two other princesses were coxswains in Regatta Day's eight-oared races in 1879.

I write the absolute truth! Our monarchs did more than sit on a throne which some persons sought to topple them from.

After sliding seats were invented in America, King Kalakaua had boats built to use this innovation. In Hawaii's first sliding-seat race, five-man crews went to and around a bell buoy in Honolulu Harbor, a distance of about three and a half miles.

Have you ever seen photos of the king and Robert Louis Stevenson enjoying a luau? The royal boathouse for sliding-seat sweeps is where the king held luaus. It's where he sang his song "Koni Au I Ka Wai," which relates to "drink up."

"Wai," which means water, was also a synonym for "gin," which looks like water. Interpret the song as you wish. I can sing it quite readily after a couple of martinis.

In recent days, the Royal Hawaiian Challenge attracted mainland and overseas crews. Sweep rowing calls for calm water, even if it is as dirty as is the Ala Wai.

Crews from Oregon, California, Australia, and Japan rowed right over the top of the muck, only to get stuck in a sand bar. Maybe someone will think about sweep rowing being resurrected on this *wai*.

Back to Duke: An artist symbolized his warmth and openness in a sculpture now at Waikiki. Duke is portrayed having arms stretched out in welcome; a surfboard is behind him.

Duke was the childhood hero of every twentieth-century Hawaiian. He was kind to me because my dad was the swimming coach who took Hawaiian boys from Palama Settlement to the mainland where these junior Olympians—using Duke's techniques— beat everyone.

Duke embraced and kissed Don Ho to seal the deal that brought Don to Waikiki from his mother's bar where he started going "big time" in Duke's Hawaiian bar.

Most everyone of our generation has a "Duke" story. He could surf, swim, sweep, and scull and was as fast on top of the water as he was in it. Duke epitomized Hawaiian pride and graciousness and Aloha!

Wally Amos

49.

The Wizard of 'Ahhs'

Wally Amos is sometimes called "Famous." He could also use the sobriquet of Laki (Lah-kee) in Hawaii. In English it means just what the Hawaiian sounds like: a person who brings others good luck and happiness.

He grew up in Tallahassee, Florida, when public schools taught rudiments by rote without creative-aptitude stimulating frills.

He didn't gain them by being read to at home because his parents couldn't read. At age 12 he moved to New York City, lived with Aunt Della Bryant, and picked up "smarts" in that environment.

Although he never experienced the sense of fulfillment that comes when someone reads to you, Auntie did introduce him to her homemade chocolate chip cookies!

Wally Amos' success in managing show business celebrities is folklore. He traveled to Baltimore and Philadelphia, which were the first places to introduce adult literacy councils.

He met Ruth Colvin of Syracuse, our mutual friend, who founded Literacy Volunteers of America. Colvin did for adult literacy what Julia Child did for cooking: She simplified and democratized a task that had been the realm of the professionally trained.

For 24 years, Wally served as Literacy Volunteers' official spokesman. He also baked cookies the way Aunt Della taught him, and it, too, helped make him famous.

Hawaii became Wally's home in 1977. In 1982 he and his wife, Christine Harris-Amos, decided to create their own little reading laboratory while daughter Sarah was in the womb.

"Ruth believes it makes an enormous difference in early childhood development," Wally explained.

"I had no previous experience in reading out loud. The two of us just spent part of the evening reading to our unborn child. It was the calmest, most loving part of every day—it became a vital part of our family life. Sarah gurgled in her crib as I read; her eyes tried to focus on pictures I enthusiastically showed her.

"By the time Sarah was in junior kindergarten at Hanahauoli Elementary School, she was equal with the preschoolers, and I was becoming pretty good at reading out loud. Sarah became a voracious reader; she gained all of the benefits that reading out loud brings to life—and I also became pretty good at doing it.

"While John Waihee was lieutenant governor, I asked him to form the Lieutenant Governor's Literary Council, and he agreed. He expanded it into the Governor's Council for Literature and Lifelong Learning. The dedicated readers at the Rotary Club of Honolulu Sunrise became involved. Lynne Waihee, former high school English teacher and

John Waihee's wife, moved this program forward as the Read to Me International Foundation.

Amos says, "Before we opened our Kailua store about three and a half years ago, Christine suggested we promote literacy. We formed the Read It LOUD Foundation and tithe 10 percent of our profits to it. Most everyone in town knows that I read to kids in the store. Of course, the parents listen in; it's hard to tell who is the most excited by the stories."

I asked Wally for some parental reading tips:

"It is so easy to do and you become better with practice. Start the tradition of bedtime stories for little kids. Only ten minutes a day from birth to six years old. The greatest gift in the world and it's free. Local librarians will suggest books that are good to read out loud.

"Go to the library with children and choose a book with them. When ready to read, discuss the story and the illustrations. Identify the big idea within the book. Every book has one. Figure it out. You can't fool *keiki*. Become engrossed, change your reading voice to identify the characters.

"Be enthusiastic, raise your voice and bring the words to life. You are on stage for the child—be an actor!

"Children and adults love hearing good stories read out loud during family gatherings—ostensibly for the kids, but you may be surprised at the interest from others. It strengthens family bonds. A little tip: Make certain your children grow up seeing you read often. Become a friend of your local libary—it has what you need for a good life."

I asked, "What do you look for when reading to children?"

"I watch to see if I am connecting. I may become more dramatic if any listener is being hesitant."

"One last question, Wally: What do you find the most satisfying while reading: the giggles? The ohhs?"

"It is their sense of wonder. Their wide eyes, the sound of their aahs.

"Children's' awe and aah's—there's nothing like it."

50.

Kui Lee: Beautiful Days of Our Youth

Kui Lee achieved his life's ambition shortly before he died.

There was nothing wimpy about high-energy Kui—whether he was being a knife dancer, composing songs in a hurry for a few bucks for celebrity pals such as Bobby Darin to use in the Borscht Belt, or going face-to-face with authority.

Would his being too bright, too slight, and too feisty make him hard to love by those of us growing up with him? Not at all; he was our "little big man."

In 1965, in late stages of throat cancer, Kui expressed lingering regret to a school friend over being unable to fulfill what had become an overriding life ambition.

"And what is that?" asked Douglas Mossman.

"To graduate from High School," Kui answered.

Kui was what Malcolm Gladwell describes as an "Outlier" in his best-selling book by that name. This is one who is detached from the main body of ordinary persons—someone who's extraordinary and has a high IQ.

Although physically undersized, Kui probably had the largest brain on campus in terms of intelligence quotient.

Quick and articulate, he learned anything immediately—seemingly spontaneously. Such aptitude was out of step with his dogmatic behavioral processes.

After a long spell, local radio stations reported the exciting news that "the surf is breaking big" at Waikiki. Hearing this at 6 a.m., Kui complained loudly of a toothache at 7:00 a.m. breakfast—he sat at Vice Principal Bailey's table. Mr. Bailey gave Kui a medical emergency pass. Mossman phoned his dentist uncle to expect Kui.

The uncle gave Kui a pat on the head and an aspirin along with a slip verifying that Kui had come to his dental office.

Kui returned to campus sunburned, with bloodshot eyes, and behaving euphorically.

During breakfast in the dining hall the next morning, Mr. Bailey saw a front-page newspaper photo of Kui riding a wave. The caption read: "A Kamehameha boy enjoying the big surf."

Mr. Bailey put the paper down and spoke to Kui:

"Finish your porridge, then I want to see you immediately in my office."

Once there, Kui talked fast; he had all kinds of creative logic about it being a Hawaiian boys' obligation to surf when waves reached their peak.

Patient Mr. Bailey sighed: "You broke the rules and lied about it—100 demerits."

"I'm leaving," he told his friends as he packed back in the dormitory. "They're going to throw me out sooner or later; I won't wait."

And then he just sort of disappeared, eventually surfacing as a regular performer in New York City's Lexington Hotel's "Hawaiian Room"—along with some of the Beamers.

Kui's throat cancer was evident when he and Nani and their four children returned to Hawaii in the 1960s.

He demonstrated his music to Don Ho. It included "One Paddle, Two Paddle," describing the sense of unity in paddling an outrigger canoe in precise synchronization. It expressed frustration with Big Cities—which he'd left behind him.

Losing patience with "Lahainaluna," while composing it on a Maui beach, he threw it in a trash can. His wife Nani retrieved it to show Don Ho who had scored big earlier in 1965 with Kui's "I'll Remember You."

Don popularized it.

Kui was the antithesis to mellow Ho.

Impatient with himself and everything, Kui could quickly turn abrasive.

It's a curse for many highly intelligent persons, I read somewhere—Gladwell doesn't go into it.

Kui shared his entire repertoire with Don, including "My Hawaii," a song with exquisite words about Molokai.

And then he wrote what may have been his requiem, "It's Time to Go."

Touched by his regrets, Doug contacted my uncle, Richard Lyman, board chairman of the Bishop Estate. "Poppa" Lyman made arrangements, and the top brain of the class of 1950 received a Kamehameha Schools graduation certificate directly from smiling Mr. Allen Bailey.

His ashes went into Waikiki's waters in 1966. Kui Lee was only 34.

Was Kui Lee an inheritor of unfulfilled renown? Not at all.

He helped create what some term as "Hawaiian Renaissance music" that Don Ho and others popularized.

51.

King and Mrs. Roosevelt's Lomilomi

A little Hawaiian-style rub with quiet humming relieves pain in souls and soles. It's something people of my generation learned growing up here.

Eleanor Roosevelt, one of the most important women of the twentieth century, often attended Barnard College's faculty teas on its New York City campus. It was Hawaii student Nona Beamer's turn to be hostess and she invited Charles E. King, a family friend, as her guest.

King, in the music publishing phase of his life, was living and working in New York City.

Nona told me, "He was so charming. He sat beside Mrs. Roosevelt, talking with her while I served tea. They appeared to be having a lot of fun.

"Then I looked over and saw him kneeling down and taking off her shoes.

"I wondered, *What is going on with Uncle Charles?* She wore gunboats—large ugly walking shoes."

Mrs. Roosevelt was famous for striding around New York City.

Others rode, Mrs. President strode!

Evidently, Mrs. Roosevelt mentioned to Charles that her feet were feeling painful. So he did what anyone growing up Hawaii would do:

He took off her shoes and used *lomilomi* on her bare feet!

He rubbed, kneaded, hummed a little song, and put his magical skills to work. He used this healing technique we learn from *kupuna*—our elders.

Lomilomi is a passive form of exercise with a little spirituality involved. I'll avoid that part of it here.

Within a short time, King was tying Mrs. Roosevelt's gunboats while other women in the room looked wistfully at Hawaii's great composer.

Nona said, "At the end of the tea, Mrs. Roosevelt told everybody, 'Are you going to invite Uncle Charles to the next tea? Oh please do!'"

The other women's eyes shined.

Obviously Charlie King had made Mrs. Roosevelt's toes sing. It appeared she wasn't the only one for whom King's musical touch seemed appealing.

Seeing my eyes gleam, the late Auntie Nona may have been chiding me, as well as King, when she told me her firm retort:

"Charles E. King, how can you be such a flirt? She is the president's wife.

"*Uncle Charles.* Indeed!"

Growing up in Hawaii, he'd learned the value of soulful music to ease the heart and *lomilomi* to soothe the soles of the feet.

It works nicely on a stiff neck as well. *Ah. . . .*

52.

Douglas Mossman: Applause Thrills

This Hawaiian actor put his lifelong career into perspective.

* * *

I am especially retrospective about life at Christmastime. That's when, at age eight, my professional acting career was shaped. Everything I've done was rooted on my experience in a Christmas play when I was eight years old and in the third grade at Kapalama School.

I put everything I could into "Why the Chimes Rang," our school's annual Christmas play. This was my first onstage performance. The curtains came down and something happened I'll never forget:

People put their hands together—back and forth, repeatedly and rapidly.

"What's that?" I asked our teacher who came stage front to share bows with the cast and to give me a special hug.

"It's applause."

Chills ran up and down my spine. My face was warmed from a rosy glow.

I asked: "What made them do that? Why are they grinning so at me?"

"I'll explain," my teacher said as we walked offstage.

She told me the story of the *widow's mite*. Sixty-eight years ago teachers could use a Bible story in public schools to illustrate a point.

Jesus explained that the widow's small gift was the most precious of all because she gave all that she had, holding back nothing. That's from Mark 12:41-44.

I was eager for another chance to do the same thing. Applause filled my inner need for approval. I felt that by not holding anything back I might become mighty!

* * *

Tall upfront, distinguished Mossman, as a mighty mite? I couldn't help smiling at that thought.

* * *

The next year I wore blackface makeup in the play "Nicodemus." I was "Nick," a black kid who was experiencing problems. I savored the applause.

Our school's total performing arts program consisted of a Christmas play—our one chance to shine.

Mother worked in surgery at Kaneohe Territorial Hospital, known as "The Pupule House." Lobotomies were SOP—standard operating procedures.

Dear friendly mother, whenever she heard the surname of someone she met for the first time, she often found a connection with a patient she had known.

She would express it enthusiastically, happy to make a link between someone she'd served and someone she'd just met.

Her openness made sister Dallas and I even shyer.

Dallas, a year older, and I went to live with mother's brother George Needham on the Big Island. He was bookkeeper and office manager at Paahau Sugar Plantation. Aunty Piilani taught at Honokaa High School.

Uncle George's children became boarders at Kamehameha School; so did Dallas and I after transferring from the Honokaa School.

The Rev. Stephen Desha, who interviewed us, wanted to jump one-year-older Dallas from the 7th to 9th grade so we both could come to Kamehameha when I arrived as an 8th grader.

Gone now, she was so incredibly bright.

Dr. Frederich, the girls school principal, wouldn't let her skip from 7th to 9th. That's why my year-older sister and I were in the eighth grade together. She attended the girls school, just up the hill from the boys school.

I was tall, skinny, shy, 12 years old, from a plantation town, and the roommate of Everett Ho, Don's brother.

Everett was equally earnest and diligent as Don. Everett died a war hero in Korea. He was an Army medic, a saver of lives—a target enemy snipers coveted.

The first night, after the bedtime bell rang, I heard sniffles from the room across the way. Then I heard crying throughout our first-year dormitory. It was the first night away from home for most of the boys.

I muddled my way through until the 10th grade, when I had the opportunity to audition for the Christmas play.

I became the Grandfather; they put white stuff in my hair. Once again I experienced thrilling *applause!*

Christmas and senior plays and yearly song contests were the only opportunities to perform—something I now knew was in my blood.

Being the leading man in our senior play, a comedy, helped me to visualize a future as *a leading man.*

After serving in the Army during the Korean War, I went to Pasadena College of Theatre Arts. Dustin Hoffman was my classmate. Gene Hackman, also a student, became my very best pal.

As a war vet, I was the oldest in our class and the first to win a paying role—as a character actor. That's when I discovered I wasn't considered leading man material.

I was cast as a wild Indian who rode into town on a horse and sprang off it to enter a saloon. I lied about my horsemanship when interviewed for the part. I'd never ridden a horse.

Fortunately, they had a stunt man who rode for me in the long shots and did the flamboyant dismounting.

After that I played a lot of Indian roles. Nonwhites like me weren't considered for leading men. Ethnicity wasn't extant as today.

I had a long run as a fierce Indian warrior in the Cochise TV series. Darker guys like me were called "living scenery" in all kinds of films.

I was just right for the *Hawaiian Eye* and *Hawaii 5-0* television series. Acting and helping to produce and direct are what I did for about 30 years.

It was a wonderful career. Retrospectively, I realize that being on-screen never provided the same thrill I first experienced from a live audience putting their hands together — back and forth, repeatedly and rapidly at Kapalama School.

That's where a first glimpse of opportunity appeared. Christmas always brings it to mind.

Don Ho.

53.

Don Ho: How to Talk with Women

What will cause grandmotherly women to stare lovingly and dance on request—even if it's an improvisation?

Don Ho's cryptic answer:

"Know how to talk with women."

How?

He demonstrated how most men talk. For contrast, he used verbal connections for which he became famous.

"Wow! Let's do a book on how to talk with women," I said enthusiastically.

"Nah. Then everyone could do it and my stage career would end."

Don Ho's communications style was pure "Honey Ho." The eldest boy of six children, Don fed the chickens, rabbits, and pigs, and helped scrub his brothers and sisters at the outdoor shower in the afternoon when the cold water was warmed by the sun.

He once told me, "My mother didn't care if we lived in a broken-down shack. It always has to be clean." It was his way of saying I'd better neaten up if I were to survive as his eighth-grade roommate. I didn't want "Lepo," the nickname he suggested I was on the way to earning. (It means "Rubbish" or worse. I wasn't up to his speed, having lived in foster homes, not with a Honey.)

When they moved to Kaneohe, Aunt Cutie and her kids slept in the tiny house's bedroom, the Ho girls used the living room, Honey and her husband Jimmy had the garage, and the Ho boys slept in the shed.

Don's dad was a charming man with lots of ideas and high enthusiasm but without the background to carry them through.

Frustrated by the Depression, Jimmy, like so many Island men, pursued his fleeting youth—roaming instead of homing. Most everything fell on Honey's shoulders.

They turned the Ice House next door into a restaurant. His mother gave it her name, "Honey's," and put in 18-hour days creating a reputation for gourmet Hawaiian food. She obtained a beer license and kept things mellow between servicemen and locals.

Honey's Café reflected Ho's mother's robust embrace of the human race and his father's rakish optimism. She sometimes helped the bouncer stop fights.

Don said, "To me, a 'Hawaiian' is anyone local. Neighbors were Hawaiian in our eyes. A gracious Chinese family across the street brought us *kulolo* on Christmas. My Japanese friends helped me rake the yard. Mother paid them maybe 50 cents an hour. One of those kids is now a doctor."

Don became an Air Force pilot. During the end of the Korean War he was relocated to Hickam Air Force

Base and spent free time helping at Honey's. He resigned from the Air Force to assist his ailing mother and became manager, bartender, and dishwasher.

Honey was the drawing attraction. With her out, they were lucky to take in $25 a day.

"Why don't you put your electric organ behind the bar?" Honey suggested to Don. "People like music. That might bring in some customers."

A bartender who sang at an organ was something new. Initially Don didn't want to move from behind the bar where he felt comfortable and safe. You may be surprised to learn that he was shy. Kui Lee talked him out of being that way.

Don's inherent sense of timing and witty repartee, and his nimble mixing of volunteer talent with his own, produced a new kind of entertainment.

Honey contributed to his success in her own creative way. She encouraged shy locals to sing—and some became famous. She was not backward about coaching Don. A lot of people thought he was drunk because he mumbled.

She would say, "You have a good way of talking. You must always remember you were given that gift."

While in high school, when many teenagers backed away from their mothers, Don grew closer. He wanted Honey Ho to know he was living up to her faith in him.

We were glad when the Honor Roll was announced: Don was always at the top of it. That meant Honey would bring a celebration feast to campus to share with his pals.

In our senior year, he included this George Jessel song in our quartet's repertoire:

> *One bright and guiding light*
> *That taught me wrong from right,*
> *I found in my mother's eyes.*

Don's ability to relate to older women and his appreciation for them came from the relationship he had with Honey. That's why grandmothers didn't hesitate to express themselves by doing a dance for him.

He knew how to talk with women.

President Barack Obama.

54.

Barack Encounter at Punahou—12/28/08
by Marion Lyman-Mersereau

The president's photo was taken on a phone camera by Isabella Gigante, one of Lyman-Mersereau's Punahou students. The back of the poet's head is shown in the foreground.

Like a stage door Johnny.
I wait,
absolutely smitten
by his intelligence, eloquence,
moral compass, calm
I want to watch his game
but must imagine his grace under fire
in the closely protected gym
as he receives a pass,
jukes his opponent
and hits the fifteen foot jumper!

We stand—
a small expectant group

J. Arthur Rath III

in hopes we'll catch a glimpse,
maybe even shake the hand
of the man who executed a give and go
with and then against Reverend Jeremiah Wright,
ran a zone defense with a race relations speech,
did a full court press on Hillary Clinton,
went man to man on John McCain,
then did a power drive to November 4.

Naismith would be surprised
at how his peach basket game has changed.

I feel silly
mid-fifties and star struck,
like a kid with a crush,
until I see colleagues
some my elders
social studies teachers
who realize the momentous occasion
for what it is.

On the roof
two Secret Service sharpshooters
have their scopes trained on us,
watchful eagles searching for prey,
give clarity to the significance
of this singular life.

Eventually the SWAT team
exit the locker room ramp—
Grim Reapers in battle dress uniform
rows upon rows of pockets

march across each side
of their body armor vests.
They carry various sized black bags—
surveillance kits and weapons enough
to constitute a small army.

Minutes later he appears
to ripples of whispers,
"There he is! There he is!"
"Where? Where?"
"There."
And I see him.
He quickly looks over the crowd
then comes straight to my friend, Peg,
beside me,
she was a year behind him in school,
she introduces herself, kisses him,
I mention that she played basketball,
he asks, "You still got game, Peggy?"
She says, "Yes, I do, Barack."

He shakes a few hands behind her,
I reach out
he takes my hand,
I stammer my question,
he does remember my mother,
says he loved her,
that she kicked him out of the library
on a regular basis,
he keeps shaking my hand
with a gentle grip,
neither firm nor limp,

we release briefly
but not wanting to let go
I grab his hand again in a "soul shake."

He keeps smiling
then moves on to outstretched hands behind me
I tell my son to reach out
they shake hands
my son grins his most beautiful grin
the moment is over
but still in his presence
I watch as he graciously
makes his way down the long line of admirers,
greets the screaming young basketball girls
who crush each other reaching for his hand.

Two Secret Service men
with revealing earpiece
and wire running down their necks
move in step beside him
their grim expressions all business
Prepared
in an instant
to take a bullet for him.

He waves from the black SUV
as he and entourage depart—
I'm grateful for the moment,
for the vigilance that surrounds this man
who means so much to so many.

I know he's got game.

Political

Democrats came into power in Hawaii in 1959,
They've have been on top ever since.
Unions and politicians rule,
Some think they're intertwined.
The Republican governor who was in office when
Slices of Life in Hawaii was published
Was an exception—
In many ways.

55.

Education: Blowing in the Wind

I asked an old seer: "Why is our school system centralized and operating as in the days of the Territory of Hawaii?"

Before returning to the State of Hawaii, I had lived in a community where local property taxes went to local schools. Citizens were very interested in how their children performed in area schools.

They received first-rate education and went to top colleges.

We had no need for private schools.

"Minds of the masses blow with the trade winds," he answered.

Then he continued:

"If you're thinking about creating change, realize this: To obtain it you must secure allegiance and understanding among citizens.

"Efforts have to be reinforced by a spectrum of information to erode the strength of those in power and their cohorts.

"Citizens can play the part of visions gnats stinging a large clumsy beast—the power structure supposed to do things retreats in fury and aggravation.

"Information about 'a different way' can encourage others to support the validity of the cause.

"Community tax dollars going to community schools, direct lines of authority is a different way: That is unheard of in centralized Hawaii.

"Sheer numbers may be able to influence politically motivated persons.

"To organize a loose amalgam, power has to be given to those who will fight for the cause, to ensure victory.

"Their objectives have to coincide with the aspiration of Hawaii's people: To gain their sympathy, cooperation, and assistance under the entrenched political patronage system.

"Use as a rallying cry: 'Help the children.'

"Traditionally no one loves children more than Hawaii's people.

"The answer is blowing in the wind."

56.

One Way to Get Things Done

I try to produce lofty thoughts at ground-floor level in a large condominium complex nestled among mature trees on a slope looking down on the Aiea Country Club golf course. It is over 30 years old and has *lau nahele* (abutting forest growth) to trim and cart off somewhere.

I have a problem today:

The outside crew arrived with their truck, shovels, and rakes to haul away piles of branches that'd been chopped down. They are working right below where I write this. Brush clearing and truck stacking is manual labor. It is not mind work; I know, having done lots of it in my lifetime.

Who wouldn't like to relieve the monotony? I'd daydream if similarly engaged.

Writing, on the other hand, is mental effort—it is difficult to do if unable to concentrate.

Case in point: I have spent time scribbling merrily on a cocktail napkin at Bravo's sometimes noisy chatter-chatter bar. Studying what was on the napkin the next day—what I wrote with a bar glass in hand—looked like the "Jabberwocky" Lewis Carroll wrote in *Through the Looking Glass*:

> *'Twas brillig, and the slithy toves*
> *Did gyre and gimble in the wabe:*
> *All mimsy were the borogoves,*
> *And the mome Raths outgrabe.*

My point? Peace and quiet aid lucidity.

Well, it is mid-morning, often a clear-headed time for me. Outside, the guys are chattering away.

Scholars describe Pidgin English as a "colorful patois or Creole." Lee Tonouchi, advanced-degreed teacher and writer, calls himself "Da Pidgin Guerilla" and encourages using this idiom in drama, poetry, and storytelling.

"Pidgin" is something the guys below really know!

Tonouchi might describe them as "Right On!!!" (Exclamation points are integral to Pidgin.)

Speaking it right requires big volume—to say it loud, and talk real fast—not half fast.

It is supposed to sound enthusiastic. The guys below sure are peppy.

Constant laughter is part of the Pidgin schema. Jolly fellows down there.

It is hard for presently clear-headed me to write lucidly over the din.

Knowing local customs for expediting things, I put such valuable understanding to work.

I grab a handful of the cigars mailed to me for Christmas.

Powerful stuff. I don't write after smoking one because of the "Jabberwocky" effect on me; maybe puff one at bedtime for dizzy, ditzy dreams.

I work my way down the cellar exit and across the field to where the crew enjoys being social—with their shovels and rakes in hand. Then I speak the magic words used in Hawaii that assure things will get done:

"I want to bribe you."

I hold out my left hand clutching the cigars and say:

"I give you these *paka* for no more *waha*."

I explained, I am a writer under deadline who can't hear his brain because of their chatter.

They want to know *where* (not what) I write.

"At the ground floor level, right over there—a few yards away." Everyone smiles, nods, assures me of quiet.

I go back upstairs.

I hear the birds singing. My new pals have lit up and freed my mind instead of making it confined.

Give a little to get a little—that's a local custom. The slang expression is *Geeve 'um*.

It's why lobbyists are so important at centers of power in Honolulu. (Although I'm not certain they only give *a little*.)

Worked for me with the outdoors guys though—I have peace and quiet.

May have started something; lots of brush remains to be cleared. They'll probably be back. Next time I'll offer cheap cigars instead of "Bribery to da Max":

Geeve 'um.

Now you know a local way of assuring that things get done.

"Waha," Hawaiian for "mouth," means one who talks too much. *"Paka"* is *Nicotiana tabacum*—tobacco. Pukui and Elbert's dictionary explains it as "A hairy annual herb from tropical America which may grow nearly 2 m high,

introduced to Hawaii about 1812—tried out as a possible industry. Plants are now growing wild and cultivated."

One version is known as *pakalolo* 'cause it makes smokers behave crazily. (Pukui-Elbert also describe *"lolo"* as "feeble-minded.") Cultivation is supposed to be illegal so it may be an underground industry. Some cultivate it "under cover" in wild land as well as in a back porch pot.

I've heard it's not hard "to get a hit in Hawaii."

And home grown is prescribed for some. But growers *no geeve 'um.*

57.

Government Squeezed

Local biases made decisions
On who worked during the Great Depression.
When government coffers were too low
Women workers were the first to go.

Next T.H. job losers were the men
Not born in "the Territory" then.
Would our Lady Governor be gone
If still under the T.H.'s wand?

Bill of Rights, vocal Gloria Steinem
Makes each an equal American.
Our Gov., being for equanimity,
Says "Share—don't just take—do that freely.

Says she: "We're all feeling the pain:
State workers, a cut, join in the game."

"Must negotiate"—Union jargon,
Seeking a form of legerdemain.

Imagined and reality thoughts
Of one brave who overcame all plots.
Do you remember "Wonder Woman?"
Confronting odds, she always would win?

58.

Hawaii Slanguage

Plain English once was the Territory of Hawaii's Educational Mandate, "B.S." (Before Statehood). Qualifying youths could be admitted to English Standard Schools such as Robert Louis Stevenson Intermediate and Roosevelt High, where teachers emphasized lucidity, as did teachers at the fine private and parochial schools.

Sometime after statehood, a University of California–Berkeley bug hitched an airplane ride to Honolulu by sneaking into a visiting political scientist's briefcase.

Cohabiting like crazy with Manoa campus insects, it spawned offspring which multiplied faster than do Big Island coqui frogs. These spread "Slanguage" everywhere, infecting most everyone wanting to sound as if they had higher knowledge. It combined slang with English.

The most vociferous infesters hung around the University of Hawaii law school and bit persons who became Hawaii's highest-paid professional writers.

It wasn't long before Hawaii's thought leaders were infected with Hawaii Slanguage, also known as "Gobbledygook."

It became the language of choice for Hawaii's politicians and bureaucrats. Daily newspapers attributed such aberrant words to their speakers (maybe with tongues in cheek or check).

Users embellished Slanguage with polysyllabic words.

For example, an editorial opinion piece about "Taxes" that was written by a well-educated city council member and that appeared in the editorial section of a local paper averaged 45 words per sentence—which is the exact number I've contained in this single sentence.

Twenty percent of the words this council member used in his essay were polysyllabic. Reading level of his total article was at grade level 22 (Gunning Fog Index). That put it within the dense, doctoral-thesis-writing hierarchy. (Worthy of someone having 10 years of after-high school or even higher education. Oh, yes, and intended for reading by someone who has nothing better to do with his/her time than to cavort in polysyllabic vapid mazes.)

I didn't understand what all the Slanguage in that council member's long-winded article meant. Noncomprehension may have been the writer's intention. It was as the Bard described:

> . . . *a poor player,*
> *That struts and frets his hour upon the stage,*
> . . . *full of sound and fury,*
> *Signifying nothing.*
> —*Macbeth V:5*

Having been away for a long time, it was difficult for me to get up to speed on Hawaii Slanguage.

And then I realized *how much fun it is!*

I began to identify users with Mrs. Malaprop of Richard Sheridan's play, "The Rivals":

Words that sound good, but don't make sense as they should.

I recalled Mayor Fiorella La Guardia reading the Sunday comics over the radio to children during a 1945 newspaper deliveryman's strike. His light touch, warmth, and easy-to-understand way of speaking won the hearts and comprehension of New Yorkers.

Hawaii's politicians who use Slanguage are light-hearted, too, once you realize they're speaking light-hearted Gobbledygook, such as this example:

Hawaii is a viable option with positive impacts . . . we just need continual tourism revenue streams to improve bottom lines.

I offer this helpful introductory guide to some of the frequently used Hawaii Slanguage. Each begins with a word's original meaning followed by HS, the Hawaii Slanguage.

Input: An electrical term, e.g., current put into a system to achieve output. It is also a device stuck into hospital patients so fluids will drip in or out of them; consists of a catheter attached to a bottle.

HS: "Thoughts."

Viable alternative: Viable means capable of living; for example, outside of the uterus. Ergo, "death" would be an alternative to "viable." Death may be achieved by shutting of a hospital input device; see above.

HS: "Workable."

Closure: Something that closes or shuts. A zipper on a sheath dress would be an example: "One zip and you're frocked!"

HS: "Close" or "Closed."

Unique: The only one of its kind.

HS: "Different," but not identified by what makes it so. Sometimes HS users expand this to "most unique"—meaning "most one of its kind." Now there is a super superlative! "Unique" is used repetitiously as an HS phatic phrase, but not to communicate ideas, since it conveys none.

Bottom line: Red or black ink at the end of a financial balance sheet. Also: Where a bathing suit ends, e.g., at Waikiki young men sometimes watch wahine bikini bottom lines hoping for a beginning. Comparable Hawaiian word for beach watchers' bottom line is *"okole."*

HS: Outcome.

Hopefully: In a hopeful manner, e.g., with a smile and expectant look.

HS: Fancy way to say "I hope." This acquires a silly meaning when saying, "Hopefully the dog will come home." Will it be smiling while panting? Isn't Slanguage fun?

Impact: Collision. Auto body shops specialize in this. "Negative impact" is having a crush taken out of a crash.

HS: "Cause and effect," although it may be said to affect. This is one of Slanguage users' favorite words.

If using HS puts your mind into suspension, consider another dimension:

Try using Plain English.

Short words were as good as long ones, and short, old words like "sun" and "grass" and "home" were best of all. A lot of small words met our needs with a strength, grace, and charm that large words didn't have.

Big words can bog down; one may have to read them three or four times to make out what they mean. Small words are the ones we seem to have known since the time we were born.

Short words are bright like sparks that glow in the night, moist like the sea that laps the shore, sharp like the blade of a knife, hot like salt tears that scald the cheek, quick like moths that flit from flame to flame, and terse like the dart and sting of the bee.

Our tongue is rich in short words.

They were the heart and spine for what you just read. Short words are like fast friends. They will not let you down. They won't make you sound like a clown.

Maybe Hawaii Slanguage users intend to tickle our funny bones.

Maybe they double speak with tongue in cheek. "Lighten up" and have fun may be what they're really saying. Maybe it's just happy talk.

Their quotes are why I hold my cup steadily while reading the morning newspaper—so my coffee won't spill or trickle on it as I giggle. What's my favorite? It's the somber predictions from politicians that sometimes use every word on the list shown here and lots more GIGO thinking, which in *HS is* **G**arbage **I**n, **G**arbage **O**ut.

59.

Read to Speak

Rising realism:
We aren't obligated
To fill our minds with "Junk,"
Or, to fill ours at all!

However:
"Mental Paralysis"
Is *not* "Polynesian"—
It's for the analysts
To explain a reason.

Discover, instead,
Values in being "well read."
Within the world of books
Is what's real and what's not.
Helps coping with your knots.

Some friends take real close looks
Finding within most books
Various dimensions,

Techniques and positions
To query, discuss, share,
Perceptions to compare.
Such insights are offshoots
Of local Reading Groups.

Librarians tell you "where"
And what books they will share.
Briefly, just like a "Tweet,"
Three places where they meet:

1. Aiea Library—
"Reading Edge" visionaries,
First Thursday 7 p.m.
No costs, you borrow books,
Sometimes there are speakers:
"Pidgin's" Lee Tonouchi,
Robert Barclay's "Melal,"
L. A. Yamanaka,
Artist Ann Oshita,
An Amy Tan expert,
Me, local pretend poet.
Christmas party, great grinds,
(Joyful chatter rests minds.)
Watercress Farm sight-see,
"Namesake": book and movie,
A "Living Pidgin" play.
Mostly, we read then say
What we think for an hour,
Take turns "being in power."

S/he says "Consider,"

(Helping thoughts to simmer:)
"Hundred-Day Dash Winner
Obama? FDR?"
Both being men of their hour.
"Lincoln's and Franklin's gazes:
Their foibles? Flaws? Praises?"

Bond with someone you see
But one hour monthly?
Yes, a single focus,
With one book as locus.
Points of view, broad insight
Helps each other seem bright.

2. Friends of the Library—
Book Donation Center,
Gives old books new uses,
Has a Reading Group too.

Read "A Town Like Alice,"
Ex-inmate told of "hers,"
We find ties to "our" books:
"Three Cups of Tea" funder,
"Kona Echo" hearers.
Multicultured readers,
Age, insight, and gazes,
Depth to our books' pages.

3. YWCA—
Meets each month at noon,
Read book, bring bag lunch.

Everyone's busy.
Do one book a month?
Being convivial
Adds to reading punch.

My friend with open mind,
Kids are gone, works part-time,
Is a volunteer, too,
Likes local cultural "dos."

Good cook, keeps a nice house,
Her cheer's good for her spouse.
That takes care of eight hours.
Three monthly Book Groups, too—
"How can you read them all?"

She grins, "TV withdrawal;
Won't find much mind food there.
Six hours sleep O.K.
Won't 'snooze' my life away.

"To read more, I make time,
My mind is a resource—
Book Groups enrichen it."

Kupuna

Can you believe it?
Once some of us were
Flower Children!

Although years have passed,
Not all of our bloom
Has faded away.

Glad now,
Tattooing
Wasn't really in—
Then.

60.

Craigside's Indomitable Ladies

Knowing many of the problems seniors in our society face, I tried contriving solutions while visiting my late mother, then a resident of Craigside Apartments, a high-rise built on the old Iolani School campus in Nuuanu.

While I was enjoying Honolulu's warm Christmas weather, on Christmas Eve an elderly woman in upstate New York froze to death. The local utility shut off her electricity.

The story, carried nationally by the Associated Press, described the deceased as a recent widow accustomed to having her husband pay all the bills. She had enough money in the bank, but emotionally overcome and mentally confused, she allowed her bill to lapse. Final notice; click! No power.

This horrible publicity led to a mandate by many state public service commissions: utilities were required to conduct "outreach" efforts to elderly customers. The federal government underwrote winter costs with its Home Energy Heating Assistance Programs (HEAP of Help, as I called it). Utilities had to identify and communicate with their elderly customers and to sign up those who qualified with HEAP. All of this was something I knew how to do.

Since problems of managing on a shoestring are universal from Maine to Makiki, Craigside's sprightly residents served as my knowledge base.

I was fascinated by their networking skills: The neighbor down the hall subscribed to the morning newspaper, my mother took the evening paper. Each read "their paper" within a time period and passed it on to the next, then it moved to another person down the hallway, then to others. No dillydally—read on schedule—someone else is waiting for the news!

You don't cook things like casseroles for one person, so food dishes and desserts were shared.

Ladies "bartered" skills: Mother was a mender and chutney and jelly maker—one of the ladies' nephews supplied her with homegrown fruit.

Another was good with business paperwork. Drivers could be counted on for transportation to the library. (For years that'd been my mother's job. She stopped driving at age 82, and local policemen sighed with relief.)

There weren't other part-Hawaiians in the complex, so on Sundays, she "went to church" by tuning to the service broadcast from Kawaiahao. She took the phone off the hook during services.

Younger, more active residents took walks together; they knew the neighborhood so I joined them. Puff, puff—it was hard keeping up with the briskness of these experienced elderly walkers; I'm inclined to dawdle, wanting to smell nice flowers blooming in Hawaii in January.

Starting with them as my information base, I wrote a book about things these single ladies practiced and added ideas applicable to those living in northern climates.

Titled *Living Independently*, it helped the elderly "stretch their budget and be safer, healthier, and more comfortable." It was supported by AARP, the U.S. Department of Energy, the U.S. Office of Consumer Affairs, the American Gas Association, and Edison Electric Institute—this was like having an imprimatur.

Living Independently contained everything Honolulu's Craigside ladies knew and more: safety in the home, cooking for one, home management, staying healthy, money management.

New Jersey's utilities bundled their statewide services into a regional edition and mailed over 500,000 copies of *Living Independently* to elderly customers we'd helped them to identify.

The book was a big hit, except for a crank letter from one guy who said he wouldn't last long enough to recoup energy savings that would pay the cost of the new appliances we suggested.

The next logical step was to encourage interactivity—to replicate Craigside ladies' behavior in Hawaii with group dynamics in New Jersey. Talking with the state's director of Human Services, an RN, serving under Governor Christine Todd Whitman, I suggested an outreach program.

She told me, sadly, "In government we deal with curing problems, not with preventing them."

61.

Lunalilo Home

Visiting Lunalilo Home this time, we applied an antiseptic rinse to our hands and heeded the warning: "No touching hands or hugging. The swine flu is in Hawaii."

Hugging had been the favorite part of last our visit.

Our 20-person audience had been seated and waiting since after dinner about 40 minutes ago. The day's program listed "Baked fish, rice, vegetables, and cake" with a phrase: "The Kamehameha Alumni Glee Club will be *entertaining*."

We tried to be, but one resident in a wheelchair wasn't buying into that. He defiantly parked his chair sideways in the very last row, so we wouldn't be able to look into his eyes and at his jutting white beard.

Two other misty-eyed men sat in the front room, another back rower—younger and possibly an attendant—sat at a table, studying us from back of the room.

Five ladies in the front row captivated us with their happy grins. We remembered their enthusiastic faces during our Christmas concert. I think *they* found us entertaining.

Director Aaron Mahi gave a short introduction in Hawaiian. The audience bowed their heads as he prayed in Hawaiian—the *pule*. Ladies in the front row joined us in singing "The Lord's Prayer." Our Hawaiian version is harmonized in Gregorian chant style.

Mahi spoke in Hawaiian to explain each of our songs. Eyes of some of the brightest belles in the front row lit up. Two vigorously and frequently responded and repeated *a'e* (yes) and *mahalo* (thank you) as he talked.

We sang old-time Hawaiian compositions. Our audience mouthed the words. The guy in the wheelchair, resembling a tan Santa Claus, moved his lips to *every one* of our songs.

Initially he was sitting sideways, to seem detached, nonchalant. He tuned in after our first song and turned his wheelchair to face us. We saw him *participating* with us. He didn't quite grin—him being too "cool" for that—but no longer did he look grim.

An especially energetic lady in front-row center made hula gestures to our words. Others urged her to get up and dance.

A'ole! (No!) she said. She sat in place, doing sit-down hulas as we sang.

One lady in the front row had the doubting Thomas look when we began. She made me think of my third-grade teacher Mrs. Gow when I tried to explain that Trixie, my fox terrier, ate my homework. Lady Doubter had a mellow look when we were into our second song.

I'd never heard such rich emotion pouring from two teary-eyed second tenors standing in front of me. The one-hour-performance flashed by.

We couldn't hug the audience this time, but overtones rang back at us from the audience—they were in the air.

Background: The King Lunalilo Home began in 1883 near the site of Honolulu's Roosevelt High School. King for only about a year, Lunalilo donated his estate to provide care for Native Hawaiian residents through an *aliʻi* charitable trust. The home, with 45 beds, has very limited resources; residents pay what they are able. It is susceptible to encroachment by those who don't believe Hawaiians have preference to anything.

Old-time trustees sold the king's land and invested in the stock market. Away it went. With limited funds and running deep in the red, the five-acre Lunalilo Home is smack in the middle of the Hawaii Kai development Henry Kaiser launched on what was once a 523-acre ancient Hawaiian lagoon and fishpond. Boy, what developers could do with that land!

Here's how a realtor's Web site describes current neighbors: "This development really is unique on the island and a very prestigious address to have. Residents enjoy a good variety of beaches, golf courses, tennis courts, movie theaters, and restaurants. Hanauma Bay Beach Park is one of its greatest attractions (to tourists). Contact me with any questions on our lifestyle."

62.

A Gem That Is Diamond

Disoriented, Pop Diamond parked next to the only safe haven he remembered: a Kamehameha Schools dormitory.

"How'd he drive that wreck up here?" the policeman asked school president Dr. Michael Chun as he examined Pop's car. It would travel no more.

Dr. Chun shook his head in amazement. He was especially fond of that man. He'd been immortalized by Pop's camera at age 17, along with a girl two years younger who became his wife.

While in a state of shock, Pop had violated City regulations: He'd failed to "remain at the scene of an accident." Officials placed him under "house arrest," where he could be supervised. They clamped "monitoring" devices on his wrist and ankle for tracking, should he stray from confinement.

Pop's 95th birthday was on September 20, and some of the schools' old singers had an early birthday party for him. We wanted to enjoy his dry wit. It's kind of fun to watch him twirl his mustache after a punch line—the way Groucho Marx used to do.

Pop has a huge fan club; so did "Tootsie," his best pal and late wife. They were school dormitory supervisors for almost 60 years.

Pop made many forever young through his photographic artistry. I was there at the beginning, buying one of the first postwar Speed Graphic cameras from him when he worked for Kodak Hawaii.

Those were the days when being a professional photographer meant using a large-format camera made by Graflex in Rochester. Being the schools' student photographer, I was able to help him connect with some campus freelance work.

Col. Harold Kent, the school's ebullient president, recognized Pop's potential to portray students in a new way—he brought Pop on staff. He and Tootsie moved on campus and in one way or another, so many rough Kamehameha characters became "Diamonds."

Their profound love just sparkled at you. They'd lost their dear boy, my friend Herbie, whose spirit stuck with them. There is no other way to explain their dedication to each and every student. All epitomized one they'd lost who now they'd found.

Huge coincidence: the Rochester-based manufacturer of the camera I bought from Pop became my client, and that eventually won me the Eastman Kodak Company's business—a big career pop for me. Unbelievably so, thanks to a start from Pop.

Pop Visual-eyes

Chaucer uses the old English words *wol out* frequently in *The Canterbury Tales*. Yes, true talent *will come out,* even in a world as "overly imaged" as ours.

Consider the photography of wunderkind Annie Leibovitz, whose portraiture in *Vanity Fair* sets a standard against which few contemporaries can compare.

Pop's inner eye "wol out," which was a gift to the world.

He showed young Hawaiians in a new way. They were his subjects for six decades. Pop didn't "just photograph" a person, he portrayed "a happening," using his inner-genius eye and sensitivities, and he included Hawaii's dramatic scenics. In image-conscious America, someone is always coming up with a new cliché—e.g., "environmental portraiture."

Pop did that first.

His photographs stand the test of time. They are not an entry into time but are a timeless experience. His subjects love Pop because his photography made them seem eternal.

Word spread quickly of "Pop's house arrest." We responded with music—what Hawaiians do on any occasion. Two singing groups arrived for a "Pop's Concert"—girls and boys.

Some of the feminist crowd think the word "girls" is "sexist," but us singers are old-time Kamehameha boys—even the St. Louis College guys among us have old-timers' smarts. (Real smarts, I might add.) The St. Louis contingent graduated before their College became modified into "School."

Ours is a blue-collar, one-for-all mentality—we grew up physically tough and personally accountable. That was the culture of Hawaii's working-class people of Pop's era. Our girls once were *girls* and they'll always seem that way to us—as they get better, not older.

They're "Hawaiian," Ms. Gloria Steinem. Don't pick on me.

Pop was situated in a nice complex associated with Central Union Church. I have favorable affinities. My grandmother lived there until she was 102, wisecracking to the end. Her daughter-in-law Jackie Rath is the resident historian (that could be residence historian, too—she knows all about Arcadia 'cause her mother-in-law lived there up to age 102—and was one of its earliest residents).

Another *ohana* walked in before our concert and I exchanged *honi* (kisses) with cousin Marian Lyman-Mersereau. "Mayan" is a weekly reader for residents—she does "Talk Story," helps them have fun with Pidgin, and discusses current books.

To fellow singers I said, "Hey, gang, look out for the *kupuna;* they may be gaining on you." I'd been flirting with a blue-haired lady in the parking lot. Nice, too.

About 20 of us boys stood and sang from our repertoire. One of the girls danced to "Mi Nei"; we studied her hands and eyes as she conveyed the story in the hula.

Some girls chirped along with us, knowing every word to every song. Then it was their turn. Lovely!

A couple of the boys played guitars and ukulele and we sang old familiars. Aaron Mahi was the pianist—it was quite grand—the experience, not just the instrument.

Glee Club president Cliff Carpenter said to Pop, "We'll sing your favorite song, if you just tell us the name."

Without hesitating a bit, he popped up: "One song always has and always will be my favorite: 'Imua Kamehameha.'"

We sang it vigorously. He nodded in tempo.

As we were about to leave, Cliff chanced a glance in my direction; my hand was raised. Responding to his nod, I said:

"I knew Pop before he started wearing hair above his lip." I think he had started to shave by then—it was a long time ago. Then I sang a short song Oscar Hammerstein and Sigmund Romberg wrote. The girls joined in on the high notes:

When I grow too old to dream, I'll have you to remember.

63.

'Last of the Mohicans'

Reflections from friends "of the blood" carry overtones of James Fenimore Cooper's *Last of the Mohicans*.

A reader, Ph.D. behind his name, who settled in these islands 18 years ago, accused me of "racism" when this originally appeared online in *Hawaii Reporter*. You figure *that* out. I offered to debate with him on the number of angels that can dance on the head of a pin . . . but, after chiding me, he sought other windmills to joust.

Mea culpa: There were narrative flaws as well in Cooper's messages about Uncas, the last pure-blooded Mohican born. I think he made a point, though.

Some pure-blooded Hawaiian friends, on whose thoughts this is based, are gone. I appreciated their sensitivity over what cannot be recovered. I close this book soliloquizing with two such narrations—maybe they're lamentations. I view these as "feelings for the past"—not unlike Laʻakea Suganuma's reflections in "Hula with Ancestors," which are also in this book.

Uncas was Cooper's fictional character. These real persons were part of my life for over 65 years. Current census taking prompted the essay—should I need a raison d'etre for exposition.

Some may have similar feelings about what is happening to the environment. Please read this within the context of Uncas' realization that what is past cannot be recovered.

* * *

Data for the new U.S. Census are being gathered; results on actual Hawaiians will be as fictional as they have been since 1970.

Pure Hawaiians will be so few out of once so many—drifting like hacked pieces of a wrecked canoe rocked by the monstrous waves of non-Hawaiians.

You hear wail about the whales and commendable enthusiasm for conserving animal and coral species in local waters. Why should they be more worthy of conservation than a race appearing on the verge of extinction?

Hawaiians once so many in number, now are so limited.

Few souls seem to care, or even to count their heads separately.

Pride went with the queen's humanitarian sacrifice of throne in 1893; by doing so she saved the lives of friends and foes. We mentally relive the humiliating loss of sovereignty over our own race and land.

Some icy souls exterminated Hawaiians from the Book of Races rewritten in 1970—they were not deemed worthy of counting separately (the U.S. Census Report lumps all parts together). A new race was created for purposes of seeking federal largesse: "Native Hawaiians."

We are supposed to be no different from part-Hawaiians, now dubbed with a capital N—"Native Hawaiians"–who may have as little as 1/128th Hawaiian blood. They can check the "NH box" in the senseless Census.

Some of us are buried alive under such monuments as "Others," or "Not Reported" in other professional statistics.

The age of plant rights and animal power calls for conservation of Hawaii's wildlife and plants. What about us? What about conservation of a human race that has died away so much in a land where their roots are so deep?

I have never dreamed of any animal or plant species deserving conservation more than a human race once tied to its ocean and land—and once so generous as Hawaiians.

Some Congressional Records indicate that the Hawaiian Home Commission Act of 1920 was designed, at least in part, to increase our numbers. Our number has numbed down from the original 1920 figure of 23,723 and with so few benefiting.

It was in limbo for such a long time. HCA danced at the pace of "slow, slow, never quick" with limited resources. Unlimited bureaucracy and very little in available mortgage money was available to build homes.

Hawaiians may vanish rather soon unless something is done.

Now political geniuses have created the new breed called "Native Hawaiian"—we can't count on any preference on the basis of who we are, or by our vulnerability. Our destiny may lie in being part of this new mix.

The relentless scientific fact is that once lost forever, not a single drop of our pure blood shall ever be reproduced with the same purity. Our number is too close to the point of zero to grow.

Eventually, the average Hawaiian blood percentage among part-Hawaiians shall become thinner and thinner until it slips off the 50% mark. Then, one day, every part-Hawaiian shall become mostly something else and the new term "Native Hawaiian" will be rather hard to say with a straight face.

So many sophisticated persons have outgrown our race and taken so much cream out of the fertile and milky Canaan called "Hawaii." Those behind us may be reduced into victims of malnutrition, metaphorically speaking.

As for revival? With even minimal numbers, it appears dim. Left unchecked, the remaining years of Hawaiians of the blood are numbered—even when we tell our young people, "You may need to choose between romance and balance."

Some of our one-time guests seem to look down on us as if they were the hosts and we are sort of strangers in our own homeland.

Sometimes it is hard to maintain equanimity.

64.

Metaphors

Hawaiian language is poetic: Words are given shades and layers of meaning by speakers' contexts; Hawaiian is metaphor and vowel-laden, euphonious, evocative.

This is how "Aunty" expressed herself in an e-mail letter, explaining her return to Molokai where she was born after being raised as a *hanai* child on Maui by her mother's parents.

Her father had died, she had two older siblings also needing her mother's care, so her grandparents raised her.

"Hanai," providing foster care, was standard practice. No child was ever *not wanted* by *some* Hawaiian family.

When very young, the writer left her home on Molokai to be raised by her maternal grandparents on Maui. They later adopted her.

In this piece, she imagines herself being an eight-year-old child back on the north shore of Molokai during a time long passed.

Aunty lives on Molokai now; this is an "Epiphany" of sorts—maybe even a story of Revelation. She describes this experience as "an upbringing of truth through Ke Akua"—her poetical spiritual manifestation.

She resolves things that she is feeling. In the old-Hawaiian way of speaking, she expresses resolution with realization that she is among passing people.

I watch the surf rolling in,
Breaking on the rocks;
This mist (ohu) falling on me,
Shrouding my being.

I close my eyes as I feel it,
I taste its salt in my mouth;
I can hear the ocean—
Oh, how good it feels!

Mahalo Ke Akua—
Thanks be to God—
It is good to be home!
Opening my eyes I see
There, on that boulder,
Sits an opihi!
One and only one.

I scan the rocks;
There is none other than
That lone opihi.
Oh, how I hunger to eat
That one, big opihi.

Its existence lies within me;

As I continue to watch the opihi,
The pounding of the surf
Doesn't seem to affect it;
Rather, the opihi enjoys its presence.
Something tells me to turn left
And look at the mountains . . .
Survey their topping all the way
Down to the ocean.

We were one:
Mountains then green,
Once with water flowing—
Loi with kalo, oopu, snails*—
And all plants and creatures
That God gave us.

But that no longer exists:
Ai, the opihi has a revelation:
Yes, I am one:
Cling on to a solid foundation;
Mother Nature gave me life.

And I continue to grow—
Yes! I exist;
If man remove me
With the right tool,
I will be eaten,
Will no longer exist:
For I am the last.

Mahalo Ke Akua,
Aunty Lawaina.

J. Arthur Rath III

Reading Aunty Lawaina's words conjures Mathew Kane's gorgeous song, "Molokai Nui Ahina," the Friendly Island reflections:

. . . The sands of my birth
The tops of all mountains
And Hina's great Moloka'i
Festive land
May I return to stay, yes, yes
O wind
Blow gently
Heed, my crown flower.

* "Kalo" is taro, "o'opu" are freshwater fish not unlike bass, and "snails" are delicacies French refer to as "escargot."

65.

'Welcome'

"We have come on a visit from Maui, Brother."

Their arms advance within each other to rest
On blade-shrunk shoulders.
The faded eyes are steady,
But the old voice breaks from bold to thin.
The flowers of speech perfume the cracked inflections.

"You are welcome, Brother."

"We are seven with the baby.
We have brought our mats to roll out on the floor,
And a whole, fresh jar of poi.

"We have come on a visit for a year."

"The years are long since we have seen you last.
The sun is hot.
Come in; the house is cool."